Sex, Drugs & Murder – Unsolved Murders In Barbados

by

Kim L. Ramsay

Ramsay, Kim L.

Sex, Drugs & Murder – Unsolved Murders In Barbados

ISBN 9798462335778

Printed and bound by COT Holdings Limited, Barbados, West Indies

CONTENTS

Disclaimer

While some **names and locations have been slightly altered** in many of the cases, everything else remains authentic in the re-telling of the accounts.

The cases recounted here are true stories and represent the actual facts surrounding murders that occurred in Barbados.

Reader discretion is advised. The material and facts of these cases are graphic and may be overwhelming for some.

Acknowledgements

I could not have done this book without the permission and assistance of the men and women of the Royal Barbados Police Force. Special mention is made of Deputy Commissioner Erwin Boyce, Superintendent of Police Graham Husbands of the Criminal Investigation Department, Inspector Vernon Farrell, Sergeant Amito Pollard of the Major Crimes Unit, and Mrs. Monie Barrow of the Nation Newspaper library.

Also, special thanks to Ms. Karen Ramsay and to Mr. Matthew Clarke for providing editorial and proofreading services; Lady Muillon, attorney-at-law, for her legal opinion; Kathie Daniel of Southpaw Grafix for cover of the book; Mel Yearwood for the layout; and COT Printery for production.

About the Author

Kim L Ramsay

K im Ramsay is a criminologist with 20 years experience, trained at the University of Leicester in the United Kingdom.

She is a Senior Researcher with the Government of Barbados and has conducted research on issues related to crime and the criminal justice system. Her main research interests are penal policy, criminal justice reform and research on violence and violence prevention.

She has carried out research on homicides; gangs and recidivism of ex-prisoners. She has also conducted a public opinion survey on crime; juvenile delinquency and fear of crime.

Kim is a part time lecturer in Criminology at The University of the West Indies where she has been teaching on and off for approximately 18 years.

Kim Ramsay is the author of three other books: *Barbados' Most Wanted, Murders that Shocked Barbados*, and *The Barbados Prison System: Chronicles of Incarceration, Death, Riots and Reformation*.

Introduction

Violence is a phenomenon that has been present throughout human history. It is also one of the leading causes of death globally of people in the 15 to 44 years age group. Research shows that men are more affected by violence in public spaces, while women are more exposed to violence in private spaces, with the perpetrator very often being someone who is or was known to the victim. In the case of women, the violence is usually a result of the abuser's need for submission over the victim. In the case of men, disputes are the hotbed of violence as it is often seen as the expected response.

Not all violence leads to murder, but in those cases where it does, the effects are devastating.

Murder is one of the most heinous acts that a human being can commit on another. The taking of a life – its finality, the pain and loss suffered by the remaining family members, friends and loved ones – speaks to immeasurable grief and heartache. Many of these acts are gruesome and chilling and one may often wonder how human beings can commit such horrible deeds on each other. Even worse are the cases where no one is held responsible for the act: all leads and investigations come to a halt and the case goes 'cold'. The perpetrator(s) appear to have gotten away with murder. There seems to be no justice, no closure, and for the victim's family, this is simply not good enough as, in most cases, the family has no idea who took the life of their loved one. The sudden loss of that person, coupled with no breakthroughs, arrests or convictions, in many cases cause emotional distress, survivor's guilt and mental anguish. For some, the torment goes with them to the grave as they die not knowing who killed their family member.

In some situations, the police are knowledgeable about who the perpetrators are, but in many instances, the evidence is weak or potentially crucial information is not forthcoming as persons do not wish to become involved or give evidence for a myriad of reasons.

Though the police may have an idea of the perpetrators involved in a violent act, a case is considered *unsolved* until a suspect has been identified *and* charged for the offence. Some bodies of research state that for a case to be considered *solved*, the accused should also have been tried for the crime – not just charged – but this is not the case in Barbados and the region. Once the police have apprehended and officially charged a suspect, their case has been closed. Even if the courts have tried and found that person not guilty, law enforcement has considered that case solved.

We must never forget that every cold case represents a victim, their family, friends, and a community. The victim's survivors are people who have never received any form of resolution and knowing that the person who took their loved ones is still free. On the other side, every homicide that is not solved means that there are persons who *have* committed a crime and remain free to commit more crimes.

Between 1980 and 2020, there have been 934 murders in Barbados. About 243 of these remain unsolved, giving the police an overall solvability rate of 74%. The graph below illustrates the number of solved and unsolved murders in Barbados over the past 40 years.

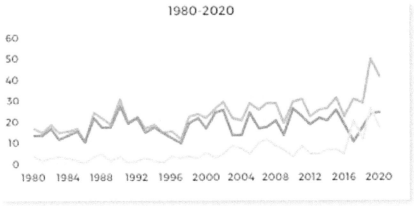

Graph showing Solved/Unsolved Murders 1980-2020

As the statistics show, in the 1980s and '90s, the rate of solved murders was relatively high with few murders going unsolved. However, the gap between the number of murders committed and the number of solved murders began widening around 2000, with an even wider gap from 2017.

Possible explanations for the gap

As more crimes are committed with the use of guns and the results of disputes, feuds between groups and gang or drug activity, persons are more resistant to assisting the police, coming forward as a witness, or giving testimony in cases due to fear of reprisal. On the streets, especially in the drug trade, there is a code of silence where persons have information about a shooting or murder but are fearful of being labelled as an informer. On the streets, snitching is the "worst form of life" and people who inform the police about crime are considered the scum of the earth, according to a senior police officer. This is a fundamental problem that investigators and the Royal Barbados Police Force must deal with in bringing perpetrators to justice. This fact, along with the small size of Barbados and the "snitches get stitches" mentality which has garnered support over time, hampers investigations and sometimes results in those investigations having to slow down or possibly cease. As time progresses, these cases then unfortunately, become cold.

Further, police have stated that drug 'lords' in some communities distribute funds in society and provide financial assistance to these people. The police have noted an increase in the families of persons who are in trouble and are in custody calling on drug lords for financial assistance for their family members. This then leads to a sense of loyalty to these persons and when they (the drug lords) are in trouble with the law, those loyalists do not offer any form of assistance to the investigators.

The Cold Case Unit

According to a senior member of the Royal Barbados Police Force, a case is considered cold when all investigative leads have been thoroughly investigated and there is no new information to propel the case.

The Cold Case Unit was established by former Commissioner of Police Darwin Dottin on June 7th, 2007, to work on unresolved cases, particularly homicides, in Barbados.

"There are at least 33 murders that have not been cleared up since 2002, but the police's pursuit of killers will go back several decades.

"We have set up a Cold Case Squad whose remit is to go back and examine the evidence and examine whatever we have on file, to try to bring a resolution to those matters," Dottin said at the time. He further said that he hoped certain technology would be available to assist the squad in their investigations.

"Murders are always serious matters, and the reality is you are not going to solve all of them in a year or two," he noted.

The Nation newspaper quoted Dottin as saying that unsolved murders in Barbados increased in the last year, with the detection rate dropping from 80% to about 63%. However, he noted that Barbadian police, like those in the region, had a problem with unsolved crimes.

"*Generally, in Barbados, we have a detection rate of about 80 or more per cent, but last year we did not do as well as accustomed and it is a matter that we have started to discuss*".

"*We have taken some steps over the last year or two especially with the formation of the Cold Case Unit, which is responsible for investigating murders that occurred over a period of time*".

"*It has had some modest returns, but to be fair to the Unit, I don't think it has had the resources that are required to deal with this matter. So, over the coming months, we are going to be putting additional resources to the Cold Case Unit to address unsolved crimes,*" he said.

The seven-member team investigated killings dating back as far as the 1970s and 1980s, including the horrific murders of Gillian Bayne, Maria Holland-Spencer, Antonio Coward and others.

Since then, the *Nation* newspaper revealed in 2017 that the Cold Case Unit had been disbanded. Dottin, in an interview with the *Nation* newspaper on February 26th, 2017, said, "*We had a group of experienced detectives who came to work every day, and it was their mandate to concentrate on these cases, while the current cases – you had other detectives working on those,*" he said. The squad did have some successes, but he admitted that this would not have occurred overnight.

However, former Assistant Commissioner of Police Lybron Sobers, who was responsible for crime, said police had not closed the files on the unsolved murders and they were still being investigated.

Commissioner of Police Tyrone Griffith recently stated that it was not correct to say that it was disbanded, as was reported, but that the cold cases have been filed and are reviewed from time to time.

Sex, Drugs & Murder – Unsolved Murders In Barbados chronicles some of Barbados' cold cases. If you, or someone you know, have any information on any violent crime or murder, you are urged to contact the Royal Barbados Police Force at (246) 430-7182 and speak to an officer in the Criminal Investigations Department, or you can call Crime Stoppers anonymously at 1-800-8477.

CHAPTER ONE

Affairs of the Heart – Deadly Tryst in the Ivy

Beres Hammond, the well-loved Jamaican reggae crooner, once sang about the "too sweet love affair," where he was "caught in the middle."

Some people thrill to the clandestine nature of such 'affairs of the heart'. Sometimes the affairs continue for prolonged periods, or they can end quickly once discovered. Sometimes, the offended partner chooses to ignore the affair or the affairs may result in breakup or divorce.

Sometimes, these affairs can end in murder.

Such was the case in the murder of Kenrick Anderson.

Kenrick Anderson and Veronica Layne were lovers. However, there was a catch. Veronica was a married woman, albeit she was estranged from her husband, Theodore Layne.

For them to have time together alone, Kenrick and Veronica would regularly sneak into the St. Giles Boys School grounds at night and make their way to a secluded spot at the back of the school. This seemed to be the ideal place for lovers to engage in pleasures of the flesh, undetected by wandering, inquisitive eyes.

Front of St Giles School

Rear of St Giles School

It was a Friday night, April 3rd, 1970 and Veronica and Kenrick were together on the steps of her house talking until about 9.00 p.m. They were both in an amorous mood and wanted to have some fun. They knew that it was not safe to stay at her place, so they decided to slip away to their secret rendezvous spot for a night of sex and fun.

When Veronica and Kenrick reached the school, they were standing on the back verandah no more than five minutes when, out of the corner of her eye, Veronica suddenly saw someone enter the school compound from the eastern side on a bicycle. The cyclist rode the length of the compound before turning and riding back to where the couple stood.

He dismounted, walked towards the verandah, and shouted, *"Hands up!"*

"What is happening?" Kenrick asked the man, surprised, and puzzled.

"You going see what happening now!" the man replied.

The peaceful night in the Ivy was shattered by a single gunshot.

The gunshot missed its intended target and almost immediately Kenrick and the man began to wrestle.

Terrified, Veronica took off running toward the nearby St. Giles Girls School when a second shot pierced the night.

After running on for a bit, Veronica eventually turned back, looking for her lover. She found Kenrick, wounded and alone, teetering on the steps of the school, where he lost his fight with gravity and fell to the ground.

At the police station a report of gunshots being fired was received and two police officers – Inspector Keith Whittaker and Sergeant Toppin – responded to the scene of the shooting.

They found Kenrick lying on the front steps of the school with a hysterical Veronica by his side. Kenrick was taken by ambulance to the Queen Elizabeth Hospital where he was pronounced dead shortly after his arrival.

Later that night at the police station, Veronica told the officers that she did not know the identity of the man who shot her lover. The police carried out their duties and, eventually, Veronica's full statement was complete.

A little over two weeks had passed when, on April 19th, Veronica returned to the police station to give them a *new* statement which was taken and recorded by Inspector Griffith in the presence of Sergeant Toppin. In this second statement, she clearly identified her husband, Theodore, by voice and appearance as the gunman. Veronica told the police that Theodore used to beat her constantly, although she was separated from him.

On this basis, Theodore was taken into custody for questioning. When challenged, he admitted that he did beat Veronica. While in custody, it was evident that he still had strong feelings for his wife even though they were separated.

Theodore – wittingly or unwittingly – then dropped a bombshell on the police: he told them that his wife told him – after their separation – that she was pregnant for another man.

"I was going to tell my mother and as I was crying, and in a passion, my mother ran outside because the blood pressure does worry her. The next morning, I went to Dr. Manning because of a headache. It was what my wife had told me plus the rumours which had caused my wife and I to live apart."

He was then charged with murder.

Having lost her lover, maybe the fear of also losing her husband was too much for Veronica. Whatever the reason, two years later, on January 11th, 1972, Veronica went to the police station, and changed her statement again! Veronica now denied that she was able to identify the gunman and complained that her earlier statement had been forced from her by Inspector Griffith.

As expected, this threw the investigation into Kenrick's murder into a tailspin and the police had little choice: Theodore Layne was released from custody.

Commission of Inquiry into Kenrick Anderson's Murder

A Commission of Inquiry was set up to investigate Kenrick Anderson's death and proceedings took place ten years later in 1980. The Commission found that there was no evidence of an attempted robbery or attempted rape of Veronica and because of the events that occurred at the scene, they believed that it was simply an attack consistent with that of a jealous husband or lover.

Mr. Reid, who was the Assistant Commissioner of Police in charge of the Criminal Investigation Department in 1972, told the Commission of Inquiry that he was not in the country at the time Kenrick Anderson was shot but, on his return, learnt that the investigation had run into some difficulty due to Veronica's retraction. He had erroneously assumed that a statement had been taken from Veronica recording her retraction of the identification of the gunman, but this was not the case. He would not find this out until eighteen months later.

It was revealed that Mr. Reid sent for Veronica asking her to explain herself. She told him that a couple of days after she made her second statement on April 19th, 1970, she went back to the station, not only to deny that her husband was the killer but also to make a complaint for Inspector Griffith, stating that he made her say it was her husband that killed her lover. Mr. Reid took a statement from Sergeant Toppin, who was there on the day she gave Inspector Griffith her statement, but Sergeant Toppin denied that Inspector Griffith used force or coercion to get Veronica to say that her husband was the attacker.

Further, it was discovered that Veronica and her husband were living together again.

Veronica testified at the Inquiry that a day or two after giving her statement on April 19th, 1970 to Inspector Griffith, she went of her own volition to the police, and both complained of Inspector Griffith's behaviour towards her and denied that her husband was the gunman. She said that on that occasion, she was interviewed in the first instance by Mr. Reid. This, of course, was not the case, as Mr. Reid was not in the country at that time. The Commission surmised that Veronica was confusing Mr. Reid with another senior officer or, possibly, that she was seeking to imply that her interview with Mr. Reid in January 1972 took place in April 1970, in order that her complaint and her statement (that she could not identify the gunman) appear more convincing.

The new development of Veronica's reunification with her husband led the Commission to argue that *"it was not unlikely that she would swing between not identifying him and identifying him as the gunman."*

Thus, the investigation into the death of Kenrick Anderson had reached a stumbling block because Veronica retracted her initial statement where she identified Theodore as having the voice and appearance of the cyclist/gunman.

The Commission concluded that without the evidence of Veronica, a *prima facie* case could not be made out against anyone. Further, as Veronica, at the date of the death of Kenrick, was the wife of the man she was alleged to have identified as the gunman (and remained his wife thereafter), she could not, in law, be a witness against him. They stated that if preliminary inquiry proceedings were initiated with a view to an indictment charging her husband, they would fail. In the 1970s, a woman could not be a witness against her husband. That law has since changed.

The police also believed that Veronica did not speak the truth when she said that a day or two after April 19th, 1970, she went to the police station, complained of the behaviour of Inspector Griffith towards her and denied that she could identify the gunman. They based this on the evidence of Inspector Griffith and Sergeant Toppin and also because she could not have then spoken to Mr. Reid on the date she indicated.

Additionally, a story surfaced; recounted by Veronica and her mother – that told of Veronica's "madwoman" behaviour on her return home from the station on April 19th, 1970 and attributed to Inspector Griffith's treatment of her. This story, in the view of law enforcement officers, was false. The timeline involved in the story was off. Veronica's mother was at the police station giving a statement very soon after Veronica had given hers and so could not have been at home to witness her daughter's return and observe her behaviour. These glaring discrepancies seemed to lead the police force to doubt the veracity of statements coming from Veronica.

In conclusion, the Commission of Inquiry believed that there was a *prima facie* case that Theodore Layne deliberately shot Kenrick Anderson "in circumstances that could amount to murder."

On the police file, there was a copy of a statement from a witness whom the Commission was unable to interrogate since he was overseas. This statement supported the findings that it was Theodore who shot Kenrick. The witness indicated that on the night of April 3rd, 1970, at about the time when Veronica said she was seated on the steps of her house with Kenrick shortly before they left for St Giles Boys School, he saw Theodore in the vicinity. Theodore denied that he was in the neighbourhood at that hour, but in the opinion of the Commission, this made the evidence more telling and served to confirm the identification by Veronica.

The Commission also noted that the strength of Theodore's feelings towards his wife was shown in his reference to her as a "*worthless whore.*" His statement that he did not beat his wife because he was jealous of her, but rather because she would go out and leave the children at home, "rings hollow," as the beatings began after their separation.

They concluded that the investigation of the case could not be taken further. While they believed the case to be solved *prima facie*, they believed, due to reasons outlined earlier, that Theodore could not be prosecuted and advised that the case be regarded as closed.

So, is it possible that someone got away with murder?

Even more scandalous, is it possible that a son or daughter has been deliberately deceived as to the true identity of their father?

CHAPTER TWO

The Rise and Fall of a Star

M any people face challenges along the course of life. Some challenges are life changing and can often signal the beginning of a rough path that can eventually lead to their demise. Using drugs as an escape from the trauma of these life challenges is never a fitting strategy, but is one that is chosen by so many. Such was the case of Julia Patrick.

The story of Julia is a sad one. Born to Elsa and Roderick Patrick in 1955, Julia had all the makings of an attractive black woman; a shapely figure, flawless skin and an enchanting smile. These features made her the envy of other women in the Bush Hall community and created a magnet that pulled men towards her. From all accounts, Julia was not only a beautiful woman but was blessed with the talent of singing. In her earlier years, Julia's voice was heard throughout the hotel circuit as she sang with her brother to appreciative audiences.

Indeed, she had a promising future. Unfortunately, that life turned upside down in short order.

From a young age, Julia started smoking cigarettes, which then became the gateway to hard core drugs like cocaine. At the tender age of 14 and while still in school, she was a chronic drug user. To make matters worse, she became pregnant at that age. She then left school and started living in the Pine. Then began a cycle of sex and drugs that repeated itself throughout her life until her premature death.

These life events caused Julia to slip into depression, and at just 17 years old, she was admitted to the Psychiatric Hospital.

Julia had no fixed place of abode. She built a wooden shanty (hut) in her mother's back yard and would visit her home occasionally, staying there to sleep and smoke. She practically lived on the streets or would sometimes sleep at the homes of various men. She had four children from different men. Her first born Nola lived with her grandmother (Julia's mother) until her death, and her last child was just 11 months old. Unfortunately, none of the fathers supported her nor her children.

This beautiful singer with a promising career quickly descended into a street character, frequenting Bridgetown, Eagle Hall and Bush Hall. She was never gainfully employed, but roamed the street day and night, even visiting restaurants begging for money and food. She soon started prostituting; not to support her children but rather to feed her hunger for cocaine. The ravages of drugs would eventually take a toll on this beauty and she became a shadow of who she was.

Theft of a client's wallet

In the early hours of October 31st 1989, four days before her murder, Julia visited her mother Elsa where her eldest daughter Nola also lived. Julia asked Nola to keep a sum of money for her. Nola refused. Julia triumphantly showed Elsa and Nola $5, $10 and $20 bills – surprising them both, as she never had any money after constantly spending what little she had on drugs or food.

Julia again asked Nola to keep $100.00 for her but quickly changed her mind, saying she had something to do with it.

"Where you get that money from?" Nola asked.

Laughing, Julia said, *"I went out by the Stadium with a man. He wanted sex, so while we were screwing, I went in he pockets and tek out he wallet. When he was finished, he start to look for the wallet to pay me and could not find it. I get out the car and run 'way."*

She then gave Nola $20.00 of that money, but then requested that $10.00 out of the $20.00 be returned to her.

Later that morning, at about 9:00 a.m., a man turned up looking for Julia. Elsa told him that Julia wasn't there, and that she visits but did not sleep over.

"I was in Eagle Hall the night before," the man explained. *"I was in a rum shop when Julia passed by begging. The fellows started chasing her outside, but I stopped them and told them to leave her alone. I decided to give her something to eat and then give her a ride home in my car."*

He then explained to Elsa that he was a bit drunk when he dropped Julia home so he did not think about his wallet until the next day. When he woke up, he realised his wallet was missing and started searching his house and his car. He told Elsa that he was frantic, as the wallet not only contained money, but important documents like his identification card and some pictures.

"The only person who was in my car was Julia. She had to have taken it."

He told Elsa that if Julia returned, to inform her that he wanted his documents back.

Elsa listened to him and realised that it was the same man that Julia bragged about stealing his wallet while having sex with him, but did not let him know what Julia had told them. He left without giving his name. Fifteen minutes later, Julia came home. Her mother told her about the man who visited and what he had said about his wallet and Julia laughed, saying "*He's de man that I carry way he wallet,*" while affirming that she still had it in her possession. Her mother pleaded with her to return the man's wallet before he called the police for her.

She quickly went into the yard and returned with a brown leather wallet, putting it on the table and telling her mother to give it back to the man if he returned. She then left the house again.

When the man returned to the house at about 10:00 a.m., Elsa gave him the wallet. He checked it and found that some of his documents, along with $700.00 were missing. The only thing remaining were some pictures, along with his identification card. He told Elsa that he was not bothered about the cash, but was simply happy to get back his documents.

He thanked her and left.

Prophetic foreboding

Julia visited her mother's home very late on the night on November 3rd, again asking Nola for money.

"*Every time so?*" her mother asked. "*You ain't frighten somebody kill you? Stop walking 'bout the road so late at night.*"

To which Julia responded with a loud laugh. "*Look, only Wednesday a man run me down with a knife in Spooners Hill. I shout at he and he run 'way.*"

"*You know who he was?*" her mother asked, alarmed.

Julia appeared unconcerned as she replied, "*No, I ent know he.*"

She then left the house, barefooted and wearing a cream short-sleeved bodice and long black pants. As usual, she did not tell anyone where she was going. This was the last time her mother saw her alive.

Naked body found in Codrington

The next day, at about 6:45 a.m., a man by the name of Austin was walking along a track in an open field in Codrington, St. Michael, heading to the Friendship Plantation nearing the highway close to the lumber company, when he stumbled upon the body of a naked woman, lying on her back. He immediately recognised the body as that of Julia as he had known her for several years. He telephoned the police and reported the grisly find.

The body had bruises on the neck and throat, and there was swelling on the face and around the left eye as though she had been beaten. Investigations revealed that near the body there were some coins and an appointment card for the Psychiatric Hospital.

Two hours later, Elsa was informed that the body of a young lady was found at Codrington in St Michael and that it might be her daughter. She visited the scene, broke down hysterically and positively identified the body as her daughter, Julia.

A postmortem examination was performed by Dr. K Sree Ramulu on November 7th, 1989 and death was attributed to asphyxia as a result of manual strangulation.

Possible motive?

Who would have wanted Julia dead and why? Was it one of her clients? Was it the man whose wallet she stole? Was it a random person who targeted her because she roamed the streets and was what some referred to as a nuisance? Or was it the unidentified man who chased her with a knife in Spooners Hill?

The Bush Hall Yard Gap area was then known as a haven for drug addicts and 'paros' (Barbadian term for persons who are heavily dependent on hard drugs). The police hypothesized that maybe one of those persons saw Julia with money and followed her as she went into the area of the stadium and probably committed the murder.

Police Investigations and Interviews

Several persons were picked up and interrogated as the police searched for Julia's killer.

One such person was a guy named Omar, one of the men Julia had been sleeping with. He knew her for several years and told the investigating officers about Julia and her background.

"Julia would get put in the Mental sometimes when she would freak out," he told them. *"Sometimes when she was getting better, she would*

get me to come and sign her out while she was at the Psychiatric Hospital which I did."

She would sleep at his home as well. In fact, she slept there two nights before she died.

Omar reported to the police that earlier in that week, Julia gave him some money to keep for her. He also saw her with other money in her hand, but did not know where she had gotten it from. Omar stated that after Julia gave him the money, she left his house shortly after, only to return later the same day.

"When she came back, she asked back for the money she gave me. She said she owed about four people and she wanted to repay them. I didn't know she had people she owed, but I ain't ask no questions."

Speaking about November 3rd, he said, *"I left home at 6:30 a.m. to go to town and I left Julia home. She was still there when I came back at 12:30."* She eventually left his home at about 5:00 p.m. *"She didn't tell me where she was going, and I didn't ask neither."* This was the last time Omar saw Julia.

Omar was unable to give the police any useful information and they released him.

Another acquaintance, Henderson, a 27-year-old male from Bush Hall, said that he knew Julia and sold her cocaine about three months prior to her murder.

He told the police that the last time he saw Julia was around 7:00 p.m. on November 3rd. He continued: *"I gave her some cocaine a couple months ago – about three months – but she didn't have any money then. I knew she would pay me when she could get it. So, when I saw her on the 3rd, she paid me about $25.00. We were in Bush Hall Yard Gap."*

In response to the police questioning about his whereabouts on the night of November 3rd going into the morning of November 4th, he exclaimed:

"Me! Not me! I don't know anything about how she died! Listen, a bunch of guys were there when she gave me the money. Ask anybody and they would tell you!"

"Did you see her with any more money in her hand other than what she paid you with?" the officer probed.

"No, no sir. She didn't have any other money than what I saw her with," he responded.

A young man named Glyne, who frequented the Bush Hall/Yard Gap area was also questioned about Julia Patrick's murder. He said he knew Julia for about five years after seeing her on Broad Street, but became more familiar with her about three years before she died. He was one of the drug sellers in the area and would sell her marijuana but told police she preferred cocaine which she would obtain from another man in the area.

"I would let her credit the drugs from me because she had a good credit rating," he said. "Whenever she owed money for drugs, she would settle wid we as soon as she got any money."

Julia was not known to have any disputes with anyone in the Bush Hall/ Yard Gap area and was accepted by the men as one of their own. Glyne had seen her with money the day before, after she had paid him, and she told him the money was to pay another drug pusher for cocaine.

Watchmen were also one of Julia's prime targets for getting business. To make her prize catches, she would visit business places under the cover of night to exchange sex for money.

Cleophus, a watchman who worked at the National Conservation Commission at Waterford, had an intimate relationship with Julia for two years. She would visit him regularly on Thursdays or Fridays in the early morning for their regular nighttime romps, and he paid her for her services. Other watchmen at the Commission knew of the sexual escapades, but they pretended not to notice.

Cleophus even visited her at her home on one occasion, having sex with her in her hut in her mother's back yard. She also visited his home and did a general cleaning for him.

He also knew that Julia was a drug addict who roamed the streets at all hours, begging, and that she was an outpatient of the Psychiatric Hospital. He told police that he hadn't seen Julia for three weeks before her death and had assumed she had been re-admitted to the Psychiatric Hospital. During the same week she died, he asked a man for her, and was told that she was seen around. Cleophus was released without suspicion.

Next on the list for police interrogation was another one of Julia's male companions, Emmerson. He also had sex with Julia regularly, and he paid every time they were intimate. He admitted going to a rum shop to drink but denied being at a bar on November 3rd. Being an alcoholic, he could provide no useful information to the police and was released.

The main suspect

The main suspect in the case was a 52-year-old mechanic named Oliver. He was the man who visited Elsa Patrick and had told her about the documents that Julia had taken from his wallet. He was subsequently identified as the person who had obtained the wallet and contents from Elsa.

Oliver, however, told a different story as to how the deceased came to be in his car. In fact, he maintained the story that he told Elsa, eliminating the sexual encounter.

"I was at James Bar and Restaurant – that is on Tudor Bridge. I was having a drink with a friend," he said. The police tried to identify this friend, but Oliver said that he did not know his name or address.

"When Julia came by the bar and started begging, I gave her something to eat – but I don't remember what it was I gave her."

He told the police that shortly after she left the restaurant, he left as well. He met up with her on Tudor Bridge and offered her a lift to her home. He said that she accepted and got into his car.

"I dropped her straight to Bush Hall Yard Gap and she got out," he said. *"I went home, but realised I couldn't find my wallet the next day. I searched for it, but as far as I remembered, it was in my pants pocket. I don't know how it would have gone from there."*

"I remember that I gave Julia a drop," he continued, *"So I went looking for her."*

He told the police that he found where she lived and told her mother what happened. He then drove to Westbury Road where he saw a Constable Barrow and told him everything. The Constable advised, *"Look, that is theft. Go straight to the police station and file a report."* However, he had little confidence anything positive would come out of filing a report as he strongly believed that by the time the police found Julia, she would have thrown everything away.

He told the police investigating Julia's murder, that the wallet contained documents, US $100.00 and over BDS $100.00. However, when Constable Barrow was contacted after Julia's murder, he said, *"Oliver told me that the wallet contained over BDS $2,000.00,"* but Oliver vehemently denied this.

Police continued interrogating Oliver. He said to them: *"When I went back by Julia's house, her mother returned the wallet. I checked it and the picture and identification card were there, but all of the money was gone.*

Oliver was questioned about his movements and a detailed statement was recorded from him. His story was properly checked and persons who were mentioned were interviewed. The police noted that no adverse information was obtained against him. Members of his family were the only persons who could provide the necessary information about him and they provided alibis. Oliver's motor car was checked for evidence in the matter, but none was found.

His home was searched for Julia's missing clothes but without any luck. The clothes that he was wearing on November 3rd were taken by the police and submitted to the forensic analyst and the pathologist for any blood stains or other evidence to link Oliver to the crime, but again no evidence was found. He was subsequently released, and the motor car was returned to him.

The leads grew cold; the case has not been revisited in over 30 years. Julia, once so beautiful and full of potential in her earlier days, is naught but a distant memory for a very few. Since her murder, those who were in that time frame are either middle-aged or themselves deceased. So ended the life story of a young woman who, though starting with a bright future full of promise, tragically fell victim to the scourge of drugs through mental illness and depression. To fuel her habit, she turned to prostitution and drugs, which ultimately led to her murder.

The question remains to this day. Who killed Julia – and why?

CHAPTER THREE

Did Alan Let In His Killer?

O n September 11th, 1993, the body of Alan Stephenson was discovered on the floor of his house.

The news sent shockwaves throughout Alan's community in St. Michael.

Since the 1970s, Alan owned and operated a restaurant from a wood-and-galvanize shed at the back of his house at a government-owned housing unit. Alan had become famous for his cooking, evidenced by the large number of persons flocking to his house for a taste of his juicy fried chicken.

Alan was well-known for his culinary skill. Alan was also well-known for his homosexual lifestyle.

In spite of this, or maybe because of it, Alan tried to lead a relatively quiet life when away from his business. He had a habit of sneaking his homo-sexual *clients*; as his friends and neighbours referred to them; through the back door of his house under the cover of darkness.

Alan's residence in a St. Michael community

Alan hired many men in the community to help him prepare meals for his food business. One such person was Jason Cottle of Pinelands, St. Michael. Jason's role included the peeling of potatoes for which he was paid $15.00. He was also tasked with running errands for Alan who rewarded him with payment in kind – a piece of fried chicken. Jason would later tell the police that he was always content with whatever he got from Alan because whenever he was broke, he could always get money from Alan, even though it was seldom more than one dollar. Alan was a secretive man. Despite constant interaction with his community members as well as his treasured patrons, very few were allowed to step foot into his apartment. There were burglar bars on the windows of his home, making it almost impenetrable. Jason got a first-hand experience of his secrecy. One day, he curiously attempted to look inside Alan's house by peeping through an open window.

Alan caught him and was furious. He ordered Jason never to do it again. In Jason's words, *"The only times I went inside Alan's house was when I peeled potatoes for him or went to the shop for him."*

On Friday, September 10th, Jason was in a nearby district with two other men. They were gambling in the road under a street-light at 9:00 p.m. Eventually, he lost all of his money and was forced to stop playing around midnight. Soon after he became hungry and decided to get some food. Alan was a safe bet for obtaining food so off he went. When Jason reached Alan's place, he realised that the light at the front of the house was off and the door was closed. There was light on at the back of the house and encouraged by this, Jason called out for Alan.

Jason heard a voice inside. It was not Alan's. Jason neither saw the other man nor did he recognise the voice, but surmised that Alan must have been in. *"Alan!"* Jason shouted again.

"Someone out there?" Again it was the unknown voice.

"Yes, that is Jason," Alan responded to the unseen man with the unknown voice, before coming over and handing Jason a silver dollar through the window.

As Jason took the money, he noticed a bicycle behind Harry's house, one of Alan's neighbours. The bicycle's splash-coloured paint design made it eye-catching and memorable but Harry would later deny knowing anything about the bicycle or its owner. Moreover, further investigations turned up no other information about the splash-coloured bicycle Jason claimed to have seen.

Early the next morning, Wade, another man who peeled potatoes and did errands for Alan, turned up at the house. He knocked on the door about three times and shouted for Alan. Having received no response, Wade left and returned fifteen minutes later, trying again to hear Alan but with no success. Wade was persistent, and returned several times during the day repeating the same action, still with no luck.

He eventually saw another of Alan's neighbours, Verla.

Verla and Alan had a good neighbourly relationship. She communicated with Alan every day, either in person or on the telephone. That morning, Verla's husband had purchased some eggs from the local egg man who sold to both Verla and Alan regularly. After concluding his business with Verla's husband, the egg man went over to Alan's house and rang the doorbell. There was no answer.

Verla noticed the egg man's plight and decided to call Alan to let him know the egg man was outside. Still, there was no answer. Assuming Alan had gone out and that she had probably missed him, she thought nothing of it. Verla tried calling again an hour and a half later but still there was no response.

Sometime around noon, the vegetable man came through the neighbourhood and Verla went outside to him.

Alan's shed was closed.

That was odd. Alan sold food on weekends and his shed would never be closed on a Saturday at lunchtime.

At that point, Verla made several calls to his house, but to no avail. She then saw Wade outside the house. He was signalling to her that he was also trying to reach Alan.

Alan's outside lights were still on. Verla and Wade both seemed to notice this fact at the same time. It was early afternoon and it was very unusual for Alan to leave his lights on at that hour.

The two then decided to check to see if Alan's motorcycle was where he usually left it, close to the back of the house where he operated the food business. When they checked, the motorcycle was still there.

This raised their suspicion and for the first time, they became concerned about Alan.

Verla asked Wade if he knew where Alan's mother lived and he said yes. She looked in the phone book and decided to call Alan's mother around 2:30 p.m.

After speaking with Verla, Alan's mother immediately called his brother and told him that one of Alan's neighbours called to say that his lights were on all day and that there was no response when she called, but that his motorcycle was still there. Frantic, Alan's mother said that she wanted to go to the house to see what was going on.

When Alan's mother and brother both arrived at the house around 4.00 p.m., they found it still securely shut up. Peeping through a section of the shed, Alan's brother's worse fears were realised: Alan was lying motionless on the kitchen floor.

Wade helped in opening the door and they all went inside. Even to laymen as they were, the horrible truth was obvious.

Alan was dead.

The distraught family called the police to report the incident.

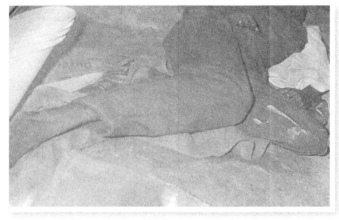

Alan's body lying lifeless on his kitchen floor

The body was examined by Dr. Lawrence Bannister who officially pronounced Alan dead, and on September 14th 1993, pathologist Dr. Ramulu performed the postmortem and attributed death to choking as a result of fracture of the hyoid bone and thyroid cartilage. There were no signs of forced entry at any of the doors or windows to Alan's home neither any displacement of the fasteners. The only visible signs of injury on Alan's body were a small wound over the left eye and small abrasions on the throat. There was blood at his mouth, on the floor, and on a piece of cloth close to the kitchen cabinet. The television set and VCR in Alan's bedroom were still there, powered on. Police checked the VCR and realised it contained a videotape with a *blue* (pornographic) *movie*.

From the investigations carried out, it seemed evident that the person responsible for the crime was known to Alan and may have been at the house, at Alan's invitation. Could it be the voice Jason said he heard when he went there asking for food? Verla recalled that on the night of September 10th she had heard the sound of bottles clinking together but thought nothing of it at the time.

Although nothing electronic in the house was taken, no money was found and a small brown clutch bag in which Alan kept his money was missing.

Two specific lines of investigation were initially launched through house-to-house inquiries in the immediate and surrounding areas, interviewing the occupants of all residences and identifying and locating known and suspected associates, homosexuals and others who knew Alan. Several persons were interviewed and the statements and records of the investigation were attached to the police file.

Wade told the police that he would normally assist Alan with food preparation and errands. On Friday, September 10th, sometime around 2:30 p.m., he left his job at the Ministry of Transport and Works and headed home. He stopped by Alan's house on the way and asked if he needed help with anything. Alan told him, *"No."* Sometime around 9:00 p.m., he went back to Alan's house and again asked if he needed any help.

"I didn't see Alan, but he shouted and told me that he was alright and that I should check him early in the morning. I said, 'Alright,' and left." He told police that he had not seen anyone in the area while he was there with Alan.

Neighbours, Anthony and his girlfriend told police that they had lived in the area for close to eight years and knew Alan all that time. They described him as a nice person. Anthony said that he would often speak to Alan, who disclosed to him that he was a homosexual. Anthony further stated that he knew that Alan was in the habit of letting people into his house late at night, but he did not know who they were.

Police interviewed yet another neighbour named Danisha, who told them she lived in Alan's neighbourhood with her boyfriend. In the wee hours of September 11th, some time after 1:00 a.m., she was finishing up watching television and was about to turn it off when 'intuition' caused her to switch the television to channel 'U', which was what was used to watch videos in that era. Apparently, Danisha was able to pick up a neighbour's feed and when she tuned in, she saw a movie of two men – one dressed in female clothing – engaging in sexual activity. While that was happening, she heard bottles clinking together and she went to a front window upstairs to investigate. She noticed that Alan's front door was opened, but she did not see anyone and returned to bed. After a few minutes, she realised that the rumbling sound of bottles had stopped. She said she heard a door lock, but she did not think anything of it as she thought it was her boyfriend.

She realised it was not her boyfriend.

She got back up, looked through the front window again, realising this time that Alan's front door was closed. She said she did not see anyone and did not know of anyone who would want to kill Alan.

Lincoln, a homosexual and close friend of Alan was also interviewed by the police. Lincoln reported to police that he had spoken to Alan around 11:00 p.m. on September 10th and Alan told him that he had a *client* coming over to see him later that night. Lincoln said that Alan never told him the name of the person. Lincoln declined to give the police a written statement.

Police questioned Justin, another of Alan's associates. He admitted to the police that he was a cocaine addict who first visited Alan's residence in search of money to feed his habit. He offered to help Alan with the peeling of potatoes to which Alan agreed. He peeled potatoes that same evening and was paid $10.00, which was enough to purchase drugs.

After that, he returned to Alan's house on three different occasions on either Fridays or Saturdays to peel potatoes, which he was paid for. According to him, Alan repeatedly hinted at a desire to become intimate with him, but he refused.

Justin was using drugs on and off and eventually landed himself in prison for theft. After he had served his time, he found himself back at Alan's house, peeling potatoes. He continued to visit Alan's house between 1992 and 1993.

One evening, he went to Alan's house and peeled two buckets of potatoes, after which he told Alan that he would have to pay him $15.00 instead of the usual $10.00. Alan told him to pass back for the additional $5.00 later, which he did at around 8:30 p.m. Alan again told him to pass back for the money, this time around midnight after he finished working.

He returned to Alan's house at midnight and Alan paid him the promised $5.00. With the funds in hand, Justin left, purchased drugs and after they were gone, he returned to Alan's house to beg for more money. *"Alan asked me for sex. I said no, but I masturbated him instead. When that was done, Alan gave me $10.00 and a piece of fried chicken."* Justin said this was the first time this happened, but after that, he returned several times and peeled potatoes for Alan. He also masturbated Alan about three more times, but he told police that they did not watch any blue movies together. He told police, however, that the only times he went back to Alan's house since those sexual encounters was to purchase chicken. On those occasions, he did not enter the house and Alan gave him his orders at the front of the house.

Justin provided a blood sample to the police, which remained on file. It is unclear what the outcome was surrounding the blood sample. He gave the police an alibi for the day that Alan was murdered, and it was found to be accurate.

Several other people were interviewed in connection with this death. A man named Ron visited Alan's house around 11:30 p.m. on the night of September 10th, where he met a man named Julian there and two other men had their food orders filled by Alan and the two men left.

Another young man arrived, and Alan then served him and Julian. Eventually, Julian left, leaving the young man there. This young man was identified as Jason, the last known person to have seen Alan alive. Police surmised there was a need for further investigations around him.

One other man, Ronald, a performer, was picked up and interviewed. He admitted to the police that he frequented the area and was familiar with several people who lived in the area. One such person was Alan. He said that he knew Alan from the time he was going to school. Alan would visit his school in the break and lunch periods and sell liver cutters and mauby. When he left school, he did not see Alan for a while because he was learning a trade.

He admitted that he first visited Alan's house when he was around 25 years old. After Wade introduced him to Alan, he started going there on his own. He would ask him if he wanted any potatoes peeled; sometimes he would get work, other times he would not.

Alan told him that instead of coming and there was no work, that he should call first. This provided Alan with an opportunity to obtain Ronald's number, and they soon started communicating by phone.

Sometime between the latter part of 1991 and the early part of 1992, he went to Alan's house and peeled potatoes for him. When he finished, Alan told him to come and go upstairs with him. He followed him upstairs and Alan told him he would give him $20.00. He told the police that this was the first time he knew Alan was a homosexual, even though he had told the police previously that he had heard of Alan's proclivities before this encounter. He stated that he thought he could have earned the money easily by masturbating Alan, but when he got into the bedroom, it was a different story. Alan told him that he wanted to have anal intercourse with him, and he agreed.

Ronald then informed the police that he had anal sex with him for about three minutes. On completion, Alan gave him $20.00. According to him, that was the only time they had sex. He claimed that Alan asked him on other occasions, but he refused because according to him, the first experience was too painful.

He told police that despite this, he would still go by Alan from time to time and peel potatoes to get money to buy cigarettes and any little thing to eat. Alan would pay him $20.00 on Fridays and $15.00 on Saturdays for peeling the potatoes and also give him some food. According to him, the last time he visited Alan was on August 27th 1993. He said he recalled it clearly because he had to perform at a show. He peeled potatoes for him and that Friday he left his house between 3:00 p.m. and 4:00 p.m. and went home.

Ronald told police that he first learnt about Alan's death on September 11th, 1993 after 7:30 p.m. Someone called him and told him about it, and he put on some clothes and went to the scene. He denied to police that he spoke to Alan on September 10th, neither did he go to his house. He gave police a detailed account of where he had been that day, which police checked out.

Adrian of St Barnabas said that he started frequenting Alan's home three years before his murder. On the night of September 10th, he was gambling near Alan's house and while on his way home accompanied by a man named Steve, he gave Steve money to purchase chicken from Alan. Steve soon came back and said that Alan was already closed.

The only person seen in the area was Justin Griffith.

Justin Griffith who resided in the wooded area near Alan, was interviewed on February 5th, 1994 for the first time. He told police that around 1:00 a.m. on the morning of September 10th, he was on his way home from his girlfriend and saw another man named Andrew standing nearby. Andrew appeared to be waiting for someone because he was constantly looking around. Justin said that he spoke to Andrew and asked him for cigarettes. A man named Shawn soon arrived and joined them. Justin said that Shawn was barebacked, appeared suspicious, acted nervously and was carrying a shoulder-strapped bag.

As a result of this interview, Shawn and Andrew were developed as possible suspects. They were picked up and interrogated but denied any knowledge of the crime.

Many suspects later, many interviews later and still no solid evidence was unearthed to link anyone significantly to the murder of Alan Stephenson. The mystery of who killed him is now nearly 30 years old.

Was Alan killed for money or did his homosexual lifestyle precipitate his demise? Whose unknown voice responded to Jason? Was Jason telling the truth about the voice in the first place? Did police exhaust their search for the splash-coloured bicycle or was this Jason's ruse to deflect suspicion from himself? Could the abject shame of participating in anal sex with another man drive a man to murder? What was really happening with Justin, Shawn and Andrew? And what was that clinking noise the neighbours heard?

Far more questions than answers and we may never know what *actually* happened around the witching hour of September 10th, 1993.

One thing, though, seems certain: Alan knew and invited his killer into his home.

CHAPTER FOUR

Of Windows, Affairs and Murder

The line between love and murder can be very fine at times and at times easily crossed. Love, lust, extra-marital affairs, deceit, lies and domestic violence are many of the strands that can be woven into the complex web that leads to murder.

The first of two girls born to Verdene, Andrea Brathwaite née Wilson, 27 years old grew up with her grandmother Monica in a Christ Church district. For a short period on completion of her secondary education, Andrea worked at several business places and at times braiding hair.

Andrea was described as a quiet, private woman who, from her teenage years, expressed a desire to settle down, get married and have a family. In 1992, Andrea travelled to Guyana with her Guyanese friend Deborah. It was on this trip that Andrea met Mikael Brathwaite, a Indian-Guyanese who was related to Deborah. According to Mikael, he and Andrea became friends. She was taking a two-week holiday and he showed her the nightlife and places of interest in Guyana. The two developed an intimate relationship and upon her return to Barbados, they continued to communicate with each other through letters. Andrea visited Guyana regularly to see Mikael and spend time with him and his family.

In 1993, while in the long-distance relationship with Mikael, Andrea met Lionel and the two became friends. The friendship developed into a sexual relationship that lasted until October 1997. This relationship produced a son.

However, Andrea was not satisfied with just being Lionel's girlfriend and the mother of his son – she wanted to get married. But Lionel was not ready for marriage, and even though he cared deeply for Andrea, he was not financially or emotionally ready to take that next step.

So Andrea continued to maintain relationships with both Lionel and Mikael.

Then Mikael visited Barbados.

Mikael told police in an interview that Andrea had invited him to Barbados and he had declined her offer because, according to him, "*It would be the first time I was travelling, and I was scared.*" Andrea returned to Guyana in December 1996 and spent a weekend there. It was then that she convinced Mikael to visit Barbados the following year. Arrangements were made and Andrea sent him a plane ticket to Barbados. Mikael left his homeland and arrived in Barbados October 7th, 1997.

Andrea abruptly informed a shocked Lionel that she was getting married to someone else and ended their relationship. What happened in her relationship with Lionel that drove her to Mikael is uncertain, but one thing was clear – Andrea left Lionel for Mikael. She told Mikael that she was in love with him and wanted him to remain in Barbados.

Mikael would subsequently tell the police that when he arrived in Barbados, Andrea lived in a Christ Church community with her grandmother while he was staying at Gall Hill, Christ Church with a family member.

Andrea and Mikael were married at the Oistins Magistrate's Court.

After they got married the couple lived with Andrea's mother Verdene in St James for about two months. Mikael found work as a mason with a private contractor but Andrea was unemployed. The couple then spent four months in a rented apartment in St. Barnabas, St. Michael.

In 1998 Mikael received his Barbadian citizenship. Mikael told police that he was accepted by Andrea's family members, although according to him, "...they were all of African descent."

Andrea's parents and some friends reported that Andrea and Mikael had a volatile relationship that involved verbal and physical abuse, and extra-marital affairs. However, they were still together in late 1998, when the couple moved to a three-bedroom ground-floor apartment in Christ Church.

This was to be Andrea's final address.

At that time, Andrea's 6-year-old son lived between her and Lionel. Kiara, an 18-year-old Guyanese relative of Mikael was also living at the house with the family.

Contrary to the reports of friends and family, Mikael maintained to the police that he and Andrea had a good marriage with few or no problems and that they even vacationed in Guyana for the Christmas holidays in 1999.

Though Mikael's recollections about his marriage were of a good relationship, several people shared divergent views. From most accounts, there was evidence of domestic violence almost immediately after the wedding. Andrea's grandmother would later provide police with a journal belonging to Andrea, contending that she (the grandmother) recognised her handwriting.

One of the pages in this journal dated July 18th, 2000, was addressed *To Whom It May Concern*. It mentioned an incident in which she found her husband and a Rastafarian woman having sex. The journal also mentioned the psychological abuse and racial slurs meted out to her by her husband. Other entries in the book suggested that she was contemplating some type of action and was asking God for strength. It was not too much of a stretch to speculate that she was planning to separate from her husband. In the aftermath of the horror that would follow, Andrea's grandmother would affirm to police that her granddaughter was about to leave her husband. The plan was for Andrea and Kiara to live with her.

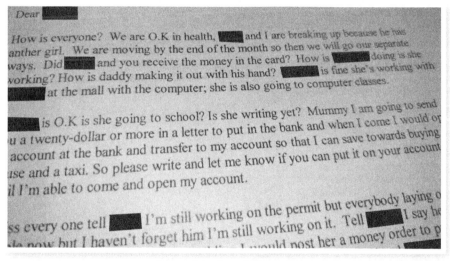

One of Andrea's letters

Andrea's uncle, Adrian, and his then-girlfriend Lizanne also spoke about instances of domestic violence and abuse in the Brathwaite household. Adrian recalled that in 1998 he and Lizanne lived at the house with Mikael and Andrea. While living there, they assisted Andrea with paying her rent. The couple occupied a bedroom adjoining Mikael and Andrea's room which allowed them to hear any loud conversations through the shared wall. Adrian told the police that on one occasion, he saw Mikael physically beating Andrea and was forced to intervene to stop him.

Lizanne told the police that she, too, was aware of the strained relationship between Mikael and Andrea and said that they were always quarrelling and fighting with each other. She said that she would sometimes overhear Mikael quarrelling with Andrea and, she believed, beating her. While the beatings did not occur in her sight, Lizanne said that she would hear the sound of furniture falling, Mikael's voice being very loud, and him cursing Andrea. At times, it sounded as if someone was being struck, and this would be followed by Andrea screaming and crying. According to Lizanne, the noises did not sound like people having fun. She noted that these incidents occurred frequently, and, from her recollection, the beatings happened three or four times a week!

Suspect: Mikael Brathwaite

Profile: He is a male who likes to dominate others by the use of physical, verbal and mental abuse. After the abuse, he tends to cry and ask for forgiveness and this was a constant pattern. He has been known to follow Andrea to her workplace, school or at friends. His aggressiveness was generally seen when he played cricket. If the game was not going in the desired direction, he was disruptive and tried to end the game.

His behaviour at the scene of the murder was difficult to understand. When he approached the house and saw the officers from the police and the Fire Department, he decided to go to the back of the house and enter the house through the window instead of approaching the officers to seek knowledge about what happened. His previous threats to kill Andrea and dump her body are of importance. He might have known that Andrea was leaving him and, because of his possessive nature, carried out his previous threat.

Lizanne stated that she was seriously concerned for Andrea's safety and she mentioned these occurrences to her boyfriend. She observed Andrea with black-and-blue bruises on one of her arms, and when she questioned her about the bruises, she would not respond. She emphasised that Andrea had a quiet nature and was a very private person.

At one point, Lizanne was so angry about what she knew was happening that she told Mikael to his face that if Andrea were her relative, that he could *not* be beating her like that. He responded by raising his hand as if he was going to hit Lizanne and told her, *"I would hit you too!"* Lizanne cursed him and dared him to do it. After that episode, Mikael would make remarks and tell her: *"Leave this fucking house!"*

Lizanne recalled that on another occasion during the night, she and Adrian were in their bedroom when she heard Andrea screaming and saying, *"Get up off of me!"* She immediately told Adrian to go and find out what Mikael was doing to Andrea. Adrian went to their bedroom, pushed open the door and stopped them from fighting. Lizanne did not leave the bedroom. However, Adrian came back and told her that he had stopped Mikael from sitting down on top of Andrea and choking her.

She also remembered that Andrea started to spend most of her time with a female friend and when Mikael found out that she was missing, he would call around to her friends or go to all of the places that she frequented. He would also accuse her of going out looking for a man if she came home late from classes or doing hairdressing jobs.

She also recounted that on one occasion, Andrea asked Mikael about a woman with whom he was friendly. This led to an argument and Mikael denied being involved with the woman. Mikael was overheard on occasions crying and asking Andrea for forgiveness as well as threatening to kill himself and Andrea would usually forgive him. Lizanne told police that sometimes she would smell marijuana smoke coming from the verandah and the beatings would generally start after Mikael's smoking episodes. Adrian and Lizanne eventually had enough of their housemates' abusive relationship, which resulted in the friendship deteriorating and the couple sought accommodation elsewhere.

Kiara, Mikael's cousin, stated that Mikael and Andrea got on well, but there were times when they quarrelled "*a lot.*" She said that these quarrels took place because Mikael would come home about 4.00 a.m. or 4.30 a.m. every morning.

She also told investigators that at one time she was home when Mikael and Andrea were quarrelling. Mikael then slapped Andrea in her face about three times and she began to cry. Kiara said that she and Andrea were very close, and in one of their conversations she told her that she was going to leave Mikael.

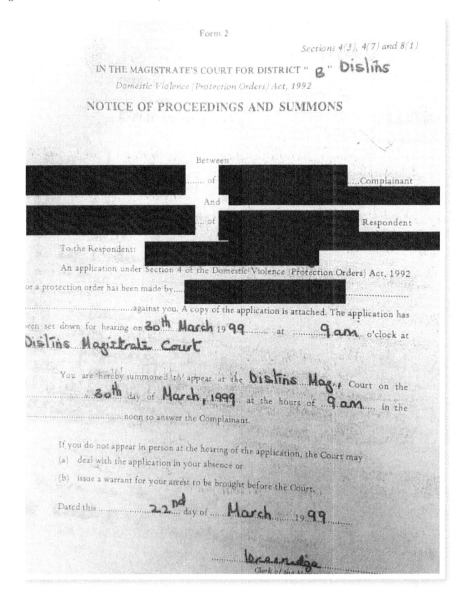

Form 2

Sections 4(3), 4(7) and 8(1)

IN THE MAGISTRATE'S COURT FOR DISTRICT " **B** " **Dislins**

Domestic Violence (Protection Orders) Act, 1992

NOTICE OF PROCEEDINGS AND SUMMONS

Between

...... of .... Complainant

And

...of .... Respondent

To the Respondent:

An application under Section 4 of the Domestic Violence (Protection Orders) Act, 1992 or a protection order has been made by....

....against you. A copy of the application is attached. The application has been set down for hearing on **30ᵗʰ March** 19 **99** at **9 am** o'clock at **Dislins Magistrate Court**

You are hereby summoned to appear at the **Dislins Mag.** Court on the **30ᵗʰ** day of **March, 1999** at the hours of **9 am** in the noon to answer the Complainant.

If you do not appear in person at the hearing of the application, the Court may

(a) deal with the application in your absence or

(b) issue a warrant for your arrest to be brought before the Court.

Dated this **22ⁿᵈ** day of **March** 19 **99**

.... **Breenridge** ....

Clerk of the M.

Protection order

After the beatings, Andrea tried to get a restraining order against Mikael from the Magistrate's Court but was unsuccessful. She said that a policeman told her to go back home and try to make it up with her husband. This 'advice' could not be verified but a protection order was indeed filed in the Magistrate's court.

Mikael admitted to the police that he was having an extra-marital affair with a woman named Denise who he met in January 2000, while walking from the beach.

Denise, who was 37 years old at the time, with three children, immediately took a liking to Mikael and they started an intimate relationship, in which Denise considered Mikael her boyfriend.

Mikael said that during this period, he had been experiencing financial difficulties and borrowed money on several occasions from Denise, which he usually repaid. According to him, Andrea's unemployed status had placed undue financial pressure on their marriage and they were experiencing difficulty in taking care of their monthly financial obligations.

Mikael told the police that he and Denise were also getting along well with each other and he kept the relationship from Andrea, *"…who I believe was a jealous person."*

He also admitted that he would sleep at Denise's house. However, Denise's mother, who lived with her at the time, found out that Mikael was married and did not approve of the relationship. As a result, Mikael would only visit Denise around 9.00 p.m. or 10.00 p.m. when her mother was sleeping. He would normally just tell Andrea that he was going out. According to him, sometimes she would ask him where he was going, and sometimes she would not.

Confrontation #1 between wife and mistress

One day when Mikael and Andrea were returning from the beach, Mikael saw Denise who had just alighted from a route taxi. She shouted for Mikael and beckoned him to come to her.

Andrea became annoyed. *"Whatever she want, she will talk in front of all of we!"*

"What happen that you wife behaving like that? I just wanted to talk to you," Denise said to Mikael, while staring at Andrea.

"You can talk in front ALL of us," Andrea said angrily.

"Alright, don't worry. I gone," Denise replied, backing off.

This, according to Mikael, was the first time that Andrea had seen Denise.

Denise went along, but, according to Mikael, this resulted in a quarrel between him and Andrea, which lasted until they reached home.

"Even though she was quarrelling, I did not pay her any more attention," he said. *"She did not say anything else to me about it."*

On one occasion, Denise, who wore her hair in Rastafarian fashion, boldly visited Mikael at his house to bring him some food while on her way to work. According to him, this was the first and only time that Denise visited his house. However, as was earlier noted, Andrea's mother reported to police that Andrea had told her that she caught him having sex with a Rastafarian woman in their house.

Entering his own house like a burglar

He continued visiting Denise at her place and on most of these occasions, he had his house key. However, on returning to his residence in the wee hours of the morning, Mikael would climb over the paling at the rear of their house, knock on his cousin Kiara's bedroom window and enter the house there. Kiara's bedroom was separated from his and Andrea's bedroom by the bathroom and Mikael explained his bizarre actions by stating:

"I did not want to disturb my wife since this would annoy her."

Kiara's enabling actions made her appear complicit in Mikael's questionable nocturnal behaviour and his affair.

Confrontation #2 with Andrea, Denise and Mikael

In February 2001, Andrea and Mikael were once again returning from the beach when they saw Denise walking in the opposite direction along Maxwell Road. Denise – in a repeat of the first encounter – beckoned to Mikael that she wanted to speak to him.

Andrea was not having it.

She became annoyed and said to Mikael, *"Mikael, what happening?"*

He claimed that he told Andrea, *"I will talk to you now and tell you everything."*

He then went over to Denise and had a conversation with her in which she told him that she was going to carry videotapes to the video shop, and he told her to go ahead and do not cause any problems. Denise walked along, and Mikael then spoke to Andrea and according to him, told her about the history of the relationship between Denise and himself.

He would report later to the police investigators that Andrea became annoyed, and remained angry until the following day. *"I had to persuade her not to carry the situation any further,"* Mikael said in one of his interviews. He went on to state that Andrea later forgave him because he had assured her that he would end the relationship with Denise.

He did not. Instead, he continued going to Denise's residence, returning home early in the mornings.

Denise's account of their relationship

Denise was also interviewed by the police. However, contrary to Mikael's account that he met her in January 2000, she told the police that she met Mikael in March 1999. They met one day when she was returning home and he stopped her and told her that he liked her. She claimed that at first she was shocked by his boldness, but still she spoke to him for a while before they both went their separate ways.

During the following month, she would see Mikael in her area and the two of them would talk. At the time she was in a relationship with another man but claimed that it was not going too well. Initially, she felt that Mikael was too young, but as they continued talking, she developed feelings for him. She started meeting him at night in her neighbourhood. At one of their meetings, he told her he was married and lived with his wife in a house further down the road. Although he told her this, she said she could not get him out of her mind, and they saw each other even more frequently.

Denise recollected that she and Mikael became sexually involved in either July or August 2000 and that in November 2000, she ended the relationship with her other boyfriend. After ending that relationship, Mikael would come to her home and spend time with her. According to her, he always left before midnight, saying he had to get home.

She told the police that during their relationship, Mikael would never discuss his marriage or his home affairs with her. She admitted that she met his wife a few times on the streets. Her accounts of what happened on the two occasions when Mikael and Andrea were coming from the beach were similar to his.

Denise told the police that one day she cooked some food for Mikael, and on her way to work, she dropped it off at his home. At that time, his wife was not at home. She said that sometimes she would give Mikael money to help out at his home and sometimes he would give her money.

Mikael's cousin Kiara

Andrea met Kiara Adams during one of her visits to Guyana in 1992. Kiara, then 18 years of age, was introduced as Mikael's cousin. Andrea and Kiara allegedly got along well and soon became friends. In July or August 2000, Andrea invited Kiara to visit Barbados as her guest. Kiara made the trip to Barbados and never returned to Guyana.

After she got to Barbados, Kiara, with Andrea's help, found work and contributed to the payment of some of the bills at the house. This was really helpful in relieving some of the financial burdens of the household.

Financial problems led to notice to leave

In April of 2001, neither Andrea nor Mikael was employed on a full-time basis. They were surviving on Kiara's salary, who was employed at a store in Bridgetown at the time. Andrea would try to make ends meet by braiding hair on a part-time basis. Andrea never sought the assistance of her family because those relationships were strained as a result of her marriage to Mikael. With little funds coming in, the Brathwaites were behind with payments to the landlord. They did not pay any rent for the apartment from April until July 2001. As a result, they were given notice to vacate the house. They made several checks to find another house but were unsuccessful.

The murder scene

The Brathwaites occupied the ground floor of a two-storey house where the landlord lived upstairs. The ground floor consisted of three bedrooms, a living room, dining room, kitchen, toilet and bath. The ground floor was fitted with sash windows and wooden doors secured with clips and locks, respectively.

In late June, a few weeks before the murder, they packed their household items and took half of them to Andrea's grandmother's house for safe-keeping. Most of the other things were stored in the kitchen, living and dining areas. As a result, they were sleeping on a mattress on the bedroom floor.

Kiara stated that on Monday, July 9th, 2001 she came home from work and found the television had been moved due to the packing-up to move from the premises. Also, Andrea had removed the bulbs from their sockets in the bedroom and the toilet.

At this time, the landlord was overseas on business.

Kiara told the police that about 6:40 p.m. on July 12th, 2001, she came home from work and found Mikael and Andrea in their bedroom watching television. She went to her room, removed the jacket she wore to work and began to listen to a Ricky Martin CD. Andrea passed by her room on her way to the kitchen and told her to cook something for herself to eat. She went to the kitchen where she found Andrea warming her food in the microwave. Kiara then left the house to go to a neighbour.

Later, having returned home, Kiara said that Mikael left at about 8:00 p.m. to visit Denise's residence which was about ten minutes walking distance from his house. According to Kiara, she and Andrea were alone and were watching television in Andrea's bedroom before she went to her bedroom about 9:45 p.m. There she listened to Toni Braxton CDs and relaxed. Kiara said that she had the window to the rear of her bedroom pushed up slightly for ventilation and fell asleep sometime after she finished listening to the CDs.

This was the same window Mikael would use to gain entry when he returned home late at night.

Kiara said that she woke up sometime in the night, turned off the stereo and went back to sleep.

Around 3:00 a.m. on July 13th, 2001 she was awakened by the weight of someone sitting or stooping over her. She realised it was a man who had her nose and mouth covered with one of his hands. She immediately started to struggle violently to free herself. When she had managed to free her mouth she screamed.

In another part of the house, Andrea was screaming as well.

Kiara continued to struggle with the intruder, kicking over a fan in the process. She said that the assailant jumped up off her and went in the direction of Andrea. It was at this point that she discovered that she had injuries to both sides of her neck and blood running from her neck down her chest. She grabbed a towel, wrapped it around her and ran to the bathroom. Kiara told police that while she was in the bathroom, she could hear Andrea in the living room of the house talking to the assailant saying, *"What is it that you want? Take what you come for and go!"*

It was then, Kiara related to the police, that she heard Andrea scream a second time.

After that, she heard nothing else from Andrea – no sobs, no groans, no sounds of a struggle. It went eerily quiet.

Kiara said that she remained in the bathroom for a while before attempting to leave. She then went across to the toilet. The door was unlocked and she went in. Kiara went over to the sink there and spat. She saw blood.

The light in the bathroom was on, as well as the light in the corridor between her bedroom and toilet, but there was no light in the toilet where she now was. When she had first run into the toilet, she heard a door open and thought that it was the man leaving the house. She sat on the toilet bowl crying.

Some time passed and Kiara made the decision to leave the toilet. On opening the door to go out, Kiara saw her assailant who had come into the corridor and was standing there. *"Don't holler. Turn your back,"* the man ordered and Kiara noted that she could only see his right side. She asked him why he had injured her, but he did not respond.

Though fear can cause many abnormal reactions, the fact that Kiara would ask this question of an assailant whom she did not know and who had earlier cut her throat seemed very strange and counterintuitive.

She told the police that she returned to the toilet, bolted the door and remained there for a while longer.

The house was silent again.

Kiara then heard the sound of paper being squeezed together and she shouted for Andrea about four times but got no reply.

Risking it once more, Kiara left the toilet. She quickly discovered that the house was on fire and, grabbing three bags that were hanging on her bedroom door, wrapped towels around her and ran outside through the kitchen door leading to the garage. She shouted for Andrea again, and again, got no reply.

Once outside safely, Kiara raised the alarm.

She went to the residence of Sylvester Greene, where she spoke to his wife Eudene, telling her what had taken place. Eudene immediately contacted the Barbados Fire Service (BFS).

The BFS responded and when investigations were initiated as a result of the report, police also visited the scene.

They found and spoke with Kiara at a neighbour's home. An ambulance was summoned to take her for medical attention. Before leaving, she told the police officers to check for Andrea because she was unable to find her. They told her that as soon as the fire was out they would look for her.

The police asked Kiara for a description of the assailant. She described him as of dark complexion, about six feet tall and short hair that looked like it was twisted or plaited in dreadlocks. He wore a navy blue or black shirt, dark-coloured pants and spoke with a Bajan accent was the description Kiara gave police of her assailant.

She was then taken from the scene to the Queen Elizabeth Hospital to have her injuries tended. Mikael, who had come back home while Kiara was sitting in the ambulance, asked her what had happened and she began crying. He accompanied her to the hospital.

In the meantime, personnel from the BFS extinguished the fire.

A search of the house revealed the body of Andrea Brathwaite in the living room. It was badly burnt and covered with a mattress. Examining the scene, the primary investigator into the murder believed that it had ritualistic elements to it (the covering of the face, burning of the body, etc.)

The charred body of Andrea

The clothes on the body of Andrea were lit first and the mattress placed on top of the body after. Both Andrea's body and head were wrapped in cloth. The Police Scenes of Crime Officer (S.O.C.O.) thought that the body was naked and then wrapped in the cloth. The S.O.C.O. concluded that the person who started the fire did not have a great deal of knowledge about fires or was in a hurry. The officer also suggested that the death appeared to be some type of "Indian style death."

A postmortem revealed that Andrea died from stab wounds to the neck and chest inflicted by the use of a sharp instrument, presumably a knife, which resulted in haemorrhage and shock.

Something is fishy, says mom

When Andrea's distraught mother found out about the clothes on Andrea's body, she told the police that she raised Andrea never to sleep in her clothes and that she never strayed far from that teaching. She stated that on several occasions she went to Andrea's house early in the morning to get her hair plaited and Andrea would be dressed either in a duster or nightgown. Further, even if she were dressed in clothes, she would not have had on those clothes as they were for going out and were not home clothes, Andrea's mother pointed out. This led her to believe that her daughter was murdered *before* 8:00 p.m., *before* Mikael left home.

Andrea's best friend speaks of controlling husband

Andrea's best friend, Christine, said that about four weeks before Andrea's murder, the house was broken into. Andrea, however, never reported it to the police as she felt it was her husband who took the jewellery that he gave her. At that time, he was using drugs, reported Christine. He was confronted by Andrea in her presence and said that the person knew exactly where to go for the jewellery, and that he saw the burglar go through the window.

Christine said that Mikael was very controlling: Andrea could only go out with him. Before Mikael, she and Andrea often partied together, but Mikael put an end to that. Andrea could not go anywhere. Andrea made a complete change after meeting him. Christine related that Andrea had made numerous complaints about Mikael and that he would stalk her if she left home.

Investigations almost immediately centred around Andrea's husband Mikael, who was found entering the premises in the morning through the rear window to Kiara's bedroom by Police Constable Carter. He was questioned about his reason for entering in that manner and stated that on his approach to the house, he saw people and the fire tender at the front of the house and was worried about what could have happened to his family.

The police surmised that this explanation was not a satisfactory one.

Mikael and Andrea were not having a good relationship and Mikael was involved with Denise where he spent many hours. He was unemployed and was unable to assist in the upkeep of the house. This led to many confrontations and quarrels with Andrea. Mikael's whereabouts for the night were checked and it was revealed that he left home about 7:30 p.m. and went to Denise's home – where he entered through the window to her bedroom – and was there until 4:00 a.m. Denise confirmed Mikael's presence at her residence between 8:00 p.m. and 4:00 a.m.

The police concluded that the story given by Kiara about what transpired that night between the time that Mikael left home and when she was awakened by the intruder could not be verified. They noted that it was difficult to comprehend the intruder's actions, the conversation she had with him and his subsequently leaving her alive. According to the police, from the facts, one may assume that the intruder and Kiara knew each other. This would account for her slight injuries and the fact that she was allowed to live, *even though she had seen the perpetrator.*

Police zeroed in on this and background checks were done through Interpol on Kiara and Mikael after local information surfaced that they were not related but had been involved in a relationship back in Guyana. However, the results of the checks showed that they were indeed related and there was no evidence to support a relationship between them.

Interviews were conducted with several persons who were identified as friends of Andrea, as well as family members. House-to-house inquiries were also carried out in the area where they lived. Statements were recorded from some persons, but no valuable information was gathered which could assist in solving the murder.

The police viewed Mikael as a possible suspect in the murder of his wife. However, they have not been able to prove it.

This is his story:

"On Thursday, July 12th 2001, I reached home sometime around 1:00 a.m. having left the residence of Denise in Christ Church. I considered Denise to be my outside girlfriend. I entered the house by the garage door using my keys and I watched television in the front house until I fell asleep. I did not wake either Andrea, who I refer to as A or my cousin Kiara. I am not sure of the exact time that I woke up. Kiara was not there as she had already left for work. She normally leaves home around 7:00 a.m. as she was working in a store in Bridgetown. Only Andrea

and I were at home, and we spent the day watching television and I also cleaned the house. She cooked salt fish and English potato, which is a meal that Andrea liked a lot.

"We ate and continued watching television and during the day, we also played with each other – when I say play, I mean playing with pillows or running around the house. It is also possible that we had sex that day.

Kiara returned home between 6:00 p.m. and 7:00 p.m. and subsequently left home just after 7:00 p.m. and said that she was going out, but I do not know where she went. My wife went and had a bath and returned to her bedroom.

I had a bath and also returned to the bedroom and sometime in the evening – it could be around 6:00 p.m. – I got dressed and told my wife that I was leaving home. She was in the kitchen cleaning while I was watching the 7:00 p.m. news. I was wearing a black three-quarter pants, a pair of Timberland boots and a blue, green and red shirt. She told me to take care. She came to the back door dressed in a black panty, and a red strapless brassiere. I told her to go back inside because she was naked. Kiara had not yet returned home, and I had Kiara's house keys in my possession. I then went to the door and kissed her on the lips and left home after 7:00 p.m. and that was the last time I saw my wife alive. (In future interviews with the police, he told them that he left home between 7:30 and 8:00 p.m.)

Mikael and Denise gave conflicting accounts of their interactions on the night of the murder.

Mikael recounted that he walked towards Denise's house. En route, he stopped and sat on a wall where he saw a friend named Jamar. Shortly after reaching the wall, a girl by the name of Marsha also joined them. They stayed there for about two hours talking and smoking marijuana. It was around 10.00 p.m. when they left the wall and he and Jamar walked Marsha halfway to her home. At this point, they broke off and Mikael told Jamar that he was going by Denise.

Around 11 p.m. he reached Denise's house.

Denise, however, told the police that sometime after 10.00 p.m., Mikael came by her bedroom window which was the second bedroom closest to the yard. Mikael shouted for her and told her to come through the back. She put on a pair of shoes and went outside and met him. They began to talk and she told him that she and her mother had quarrelled over him and she would have to look for somewhere to go. They continued talking until after 11:00 p.m. at which time her brother Brian left home. The rain started to drizzle and she told Mikael to come inside the house, but he initially refused. The rain got heavier and she persuaded Mikael to come inside. They entered the house through the back door and went straight into her bedroom. While there, she gave Mikael something to eat and then went and took a bath, leaving him in the bedroom. She returned to the bedroom two minutes later and Mikael was still there watching television. They then watched television together until Mikael drifted off to sleep. When the television show went off, she inserted a videocassette and watched videos alone until she drifted off to sleep. She stated that before she went off to sleep, Mikael was already asleep and snoring. Her daughter was at the end of the bed, Mikael was in the middle and she was at the other end.

When she awoke later in the night, the clock on the video was showing 2:38 a.m. Her daughter then called to her and touched her. She reached out and touched her daughter and found she was sweating. She then turned the fan on and directed it on her daughter. A little while later, Mikael woke up and called out to her and she fondled him until her hands got tired and she got off the bed and he went down on the bottom of the bed where he stood for a while. (Mikael's account to the police, however, was that he had sex with Denise.)

Denise said after, he then came back into the bed and hugged her up. She looked at the time on the video and it was 3:58 a.m.

Exiting through the bedroom window

According to Denise, at 4:08 a.m., Mikael got up from next to her, put on his clothes and told her that he was going home. He then went through her bedroom window and closed it. She got up and latched the window and went back to bed.

However, Mikael told the police that he left her house around 3:45 a.m. He said he did not remember what exit he used, as he usually went through her bedroom window or the back door. He tried not to disturb her mother as she did not like him.

He said he headed down the hill from Denise and on reaching the bottom of the hill, he walked straight onto the pasture and headed to his house from the back of the pasture. On approaching the house, he saw an ambulance in front of his neighbour's house, which was to the left of his house. He also saw a fire truck flashing blue and red lights and a police vehicle in front of his house.

When he saw the vehicles, he panicked and wondered what had happened at the house. Instead of going to see what had happened, he started to walk quickly through a track that led to the back of the paling situated to the rear of his home. When he reached the paling, which was about six feet tall, he climbed over it, went to his bedroom window, looked through it, knocked and started shouting for "**A**," but heard no reply. He admitted that the bedroom window was always open and that he had used that window previously to get inside when he did not have his house key. Thick clouds of smoke filled the place and the television was showing fuzzily.

He went to Kiara's room, took off his shoes, and as he pushed up the window, he saw smoke in the room and observed that the mattress on the floor was burnt. He climbed through and saw no one in the room.

He ran to his bedroom and, again, saw no one. He then ran through the corridor, through the house, through the garage towards the roadway when he saw a police officer with a torchlight in his hand, focusing the beam on him.

"Come here," the policeman ordered.

"What happened?" Mikael asked.

Again the policeman told Mikael to come towards him. Mikael obeyed and was directed to the rear of the fire truck. There, the officer searched him and asked him who he was. Mikael gave his name and was then asked who lived in the house, to which he replied that he, his wife and his cousin lived there. The police officer asked him for his wife's name, and he told him. The officer told him that his wife was deceased, but Mikael did not know what he meant and asked him what he meant by *diseased*. The police officer told him that he did not mean "diseased," and then explained to him what "deceased" meant and that his wife was dead.

Mikael claimed that he was unable to speak, and could not breathe. His stomach started to ache and he stooped down. The officer then helped him up and told him that his cousin Kiara was by the ambulance and he went to Kiara's side. He said he was crying. On reaching the ambulance, he saw Kiara sitting with her neck bandaged. He asked Kiara what happened, and Kiara told him that when she caught herself, someone was on top of her in her bed with their hands to her throat. She told him that she started to scream, and the man told her not to scream. She screamed anyway and the man cut her across her neck.

She told him that Andrea woke up and started screaming and the man jumped off of her and ran to Andrea. Kiara retold the account she gave to the police. He left with Kiara to look for Andrea at the hospital, as he did not see Andrea's body at the house. On reaching the hospital, he enquired of the police as to where Andrea's body was as he wanted to see her. They told him that her body was not there, and he was then taken into custody and transported from the hospital to the Oistins police station where he was interviewed about the murder of his wife. He would later lament that he had never seen Andrea's body, not even at the funeral.

When questioned about Andrea's murder, Mikael told the police that he did not kill his wife, nor does he know who did. He admitted to slapping Andrea in her face in the past and that they had their arguments, but said that he loved his wife and did not murder her.

When interviewed, Denise said after Mikael left her house, she remained awake until about 5:30 a.m. and then drifted off to sleep. She awoke around 8:00 a.m. to the telephone ringing and it was for her.

"Denise, you know that your friend gone to the hospital?" the voice on the telephone asked.

She said, *"What friend?"*

"The Guyanese fellow," the person said.

Denise asked what had happened and was told that someone had told her (the caller) that someone had cut Mikael's wife's throat and that he went to the hospital. She said she hung up the phone and remained at home. Later, she received a telephone call from the police. She went to the Oistins police station where she was interviewed and gave the police a statement. She denied that Mikael left her house at any time during the time he was there. She denied asking Mikael to leave his wife, nor did Mikael tell her that he was going to leave his wife. She said that during her relationship with Mikael, he never hit her or was violent towards her.

Was Mikael related to a passport racket?

Police discovered what they believed was a possible passport racket that might have been connected to Mikael. During their investigations, a passport belonging to Anthony Nicholson was discovered at the Brathwaite residence. Nicholson was a member of the Barbados Defence Force (BDF) and travelled extensively throughout the Caribbean, representing the BDF in athletics.

It is the custom in the army to have a valid passport in your possession at all times. As a result, Nicholson said that he kept it in his locker at work. He recalled that the last time he had used the passport was when he visited Jamaica.

Anthony Nicholson was interviewed about this matter and the whereabouts of his passport. He claimed that he kept his passport in his locker at work and the last time he saw it was between January and February 2001 when there was a barracks inspection on base. However, he admitted that he did not always have his passport secured and therefore, anyone at the BDF could have accessed his locker.

Sometime after this, he made a check for his passport because he had intended to travel overseas. Nicholson could not find the passport. He made another check through the barracks, but it was not found. He also informed police that another colleague also had his passport stolen around the same time and, to his knowledge, it was never recovered. Nicholson never made an official report to the police or his superiors because, according to him, he was afraid of the disciplinary action that might have been taken against him.

Police contacted Nicholson and informed him that during an investigation into the murder of Andrea Brathwaite, his passport book was found at the scene of the murder. There is no evidence to suggest how this passport would have come into Andrea's possession because Nicholson told the police that he did not know Andrea. His whereabouts for the night were checked and the search revealed that he was on duty at the BDF.

Further inquiries into Andrea's murder homed in on the close-knit Christ Church community and surrounding areas, with numerous persons being interviewed. However, little information of significance was gleaned.

A burglary had occurred at the Brathwaite's residence on January 26, 2001, where jewellery with an estimated value of Barbados $3,830.00 was stolen.

After Andrea's murder, some residents in the area said that they were hearing some people of the district saying that Mikael was seen behind the paling the morning of the incident. However, no one could (or would) say definitively that it was Mikael as the area was dark.

No known motive was established for Andrea's murder. However, the motive that was being pursued by the police was the breakdown in the marriage of Mikael and Andrea and the fact that she intended to leave him and return to her family home. The motive was under consideration because Andrea had no intentions of continuing the marriage with Mikael. This was borne out through interviews with the family members and Kiara, and also the fact that she did not inform Mikael that she was going back to live with her family. The only discussion was that they had to leave the house at the landlord's request.

Police concluded that Mikael was not telling the full truth as Mikael, in his statement to the police, said, *"I have not inflicted any injuries on my wife during the period of time that I know her."*

Andrea's best friend's story

Christine, Andrea's best friend, who grew up with her from school days and who even lived with her for a brief time, painted an entirely different story of the relationship with Mikael. She revealed that Mikael was a drug user, was very controlling over Andrea's movements and stalked her if she left home.

According to Christine, Andrea loved her husband and would do anything to please him. She made complaints that Mikael had beaten her on more than one occasion. She also mentioned that she wanted to separate from him and go back to her grandmother's house. Christine also recounted that Andrea had told her that over an undefined period, Mikael had slapped her in her face, pushed her and even placed his hands around her neck.

Andrea told her friend that Mikael was smoking and selling *weed* while liming on the block in the community. He was also taking up the jewellery that belonged to them and she believed that he was selling them. She also stated that money was an issue and that they were about to be evicted from the house which they rented. Andrea indicated that she was forced to borrow money from family and friends to pay the bills. She also told Christine that Mikael was having sex with a girl who lived in a nearby community and that the girl was pregnant.

Christine's allegations of physical abuse were confirmed by Andrea's mother.

Andrea had applied for a protection order against her husband in 1999 and outlined the same accusations. She accused Mikael of being abusive to her both verbally and physically, and also claimed that he threatened to kill her and dump her body in a well where she would not be found. In the application, specific reference was made to an altercation on March 13th, 1999 in which she claimed Mikael slapped her and started choking her and she was forced to flee her home.

Yet, she never left and stayed with him until her untimely passing two years later.

Why did she stay? Was it because she feared him? These questions may never be answered satisfactorily.

In 2003, Christine applied to join the Barbados Defence Force (BDF) and met Anthony Nicholson. She was interviewed by the police since joining the BDF and asked if she knew anything about Anthony and Andrea knowing each other. She told them that she was unsure if he knew Andrea. Sometime later, however, she saw Anthony on base at St Ann's Fort and asked him if he knew Andrea.

He said he knew her through her husband.

He did not go into any details but said it was a terrible way to die and showed sympathy. He mentioned Mikael's name to her and pronounced it correctly, so she assumed that he did indeed know him.

The question W*hy?* is always part of any investigation but unless answered satisfactorily, it becomes the bugbear for investigators. *Why?* – or *why not?* – can be appended to many noteworthy aspects of this murder case:

- The police did not believe that Kiara was being completely truthful.
- Andrea removed bulbs from the socket in the toilet and bedrooms a few days before she died.
- Police investigations revealed that on the day of the murder, Kiara locked the door from the bathroom to the kitchen and removed the keys when she returned from her friend's house. She never mentioned where she put them.
- Kiara struggled and was cut on either side of her neck, but was otherwise left alone.
- She claimed that she heard Andrea screaming when she herself screamed, but the man left her and went towards Andrea.
- Kiara did not see a knife, yet she never tried to run out of the house, choosing instead to hide in a bathroom.

- She remained there until Andrea was killed and all the mattresses set on fire.
- She ran to the same kitchen door which she had locked earlier.

The questions would not stop there. Where were the keys to the door between the bathroom and kitchen? How was door opened? Why didn't Kiara speak about the window which was usually left open for Mikael? A strange omission especially when it appeared that this window was the access route of the murderer.

What about Kiara's statement that Andrea and Mikael were playing with each other when she came home on the night. Andrea's mother does not believe this account since, in her opinion, Andrea and Mikael never played with each other. It is more likely they were fighting as was often the case.

Interestingly, Kiara left Barbados shortly after her release from the police. Why the haste?

Denise said that she received a call from a female whose voice sounded familiar and who had told her what happened to Mikael's wife. She never disclosed who this caller was and police investigators never explored this.

Crucially, the murder weapon was never found.

Andrea's mother believes that the police investigators did not investigate the case thoroughly. She stated that the police did not check the well in the yard of the crime scene where her daughter was killed. She opined that if Andrea was stabbed with a knife, then the killer might have thrown it in the well. Her mother was also of the opinion that Mikael beat her daughter for sex. She highlighted the fact that he was unemployed and was a drug user, namely marijuana. Andrea had also indicated to her mother that she was going to leave her husband and that Mikael was a sex maniac.

Was Mikael's association with Anthony Nicholson and the 'missing' passport ever delved into?

All murders start out as horrific. Unfortunately, they can only develop as *more* horrific – never less – as evidence comes to light. Stabbed multiple times and set afire, "horrific" aptly describes the murder of Andrea Brathwaite, which is rendered all the more disturbing by a failure to bring her murderer to justice.

Who do you think killed Andrea? Who do you think had the motive and the opportunity? Whatever your thoughts, remember the police can not be contented with just 'thoughts'. For them, there must be enough evidence to satisfy the burden of proof.

Two decades have passed since this tragedy and most of the persons involved with the case have moved on with their lives. As for Andrea's mother, still alive at the time of writing, she longs for justice for her beloved daughter and grandson.

CHAPTER FIVE

Terror in Lovers' Lane

P arking out in *lovers' lanes*, on beaches, secluded rural areas, or dark deserted roads at nighttime, has long been a popular pastime for lovers. Due to the typically isolated nature of some of these areas, they provide the ideal settings for wild and adventurous romance, particularly for young couples.

However, poor lighting and seclusion – so often the prime features of lovers' lanes - make these outdoor love-making venues prime targets for criminals. Despite the many warnings over the decades, and as risky as it is, many still put themselves in jeopardy of being victims of physical violence to satisfy their sexual desires.

Love seemed to be in the air for 32-year-old Ian and his 18-year-old partner Wanda. Ian was a slim, handsome man with a light-brown complexion. He was described as a respectable, outgoing, no-nonsense man. The two lived in neighbouring communities and had been dating for a few months. After work, typical evenings for them saw the two spending a lot of time together. This would often end in hot, steamy sex in cart roads or sparsely populated neighbourhoods, under the cover of darkness and away from prying eyes.

Or so they thought. Unknown to the couple, one of the areas where they would choose to park was, pardon the pun, a hotbed for aggravated robberies. Reports included accounts of victims being made to strip before being robbed or forced to engage in degrading acts in what appeared as a twisted form of depravity and pleasure for the robbers. The police were aware of the hotspot and periodically patrolled the area.

It was in January - a Friday night - and just like any other typical night for the couple, the plan was to get something to eat and spend some time together. Ian was off from work and would pick up Wanda before heading out for food.

That *was* the plan but instead, it turned into a night of terror.

Close to midnight, Ian collected Wanda from her home in his car and they headed to a popular hangout spot to get something to eat. They did not intend to park out that night, but spontaneity kicked in and they drove to a deserted area where houses were under construction.

After talking for about ten minutes, the couple locked up the vehicle and moved into the back seat. They pushed both front seats forward and, leaving the windows slightly cracked open for ventilation, they made love. Afterwards, they put back on their clothes and sat talking for a while.

Suddenly there was a loud crash!

Stunned, the couple then realised that a huge rock was on the dashboard and the right-side driver's window was shattered! From the dimly reflected light of the sky, Wanda saw the shadowy outlines of two men. One man went to the front left passenger window and the other to the right side. Both men proceeded to shine bright torchlights into the vehicles, directly into their eyes, temporarily blinding them. As Ian and Wanda raised their hands instinctively to shield their eyes from piercing beams, they were able to see that both men were armed with guns. The man at the shattered driver's window proceeded to clear the shards of glass from the window with his torchlight.

He then pointed the gun he was holding at Ian and Wanda. At the sight of the gun, Ian gasped loudly and settled back, but Wanda started to cry hysterically. Reality hit them that they were in the middle of a deserted area staring down the barrels of two guns held by two gunmen. To describe their position as vulnerable was an understatement and shouting was pointless as there was no one around to hear them.

This was a life-or-death situation and how they responded was what mattered. The important thing was to think quickly and logically and be observant. With no good options, the couple was faced with a tough decision: to fight or give in to the prowlers.

Wanda, who was on the left side of the back seat, observed that the man on the right (Gunman R) was wearing a greyish-blue, long-sleeved, pullover hooded sweater, and white wrist-length gloves with a red stripe on the sides. Over his head he wore a greyish coloured full-face ski mask with one large oval opening for both eyes and another hole for the mouth. The ski mask came with an attached knitted hat. Gunman R fidgeted a lot with his sleeves.

The man on the left (Gunman L) wore a black tee-shirt, shades and his hair was plaited back in cornrows. Both men were dark in complexion.

Gunman R, who did all the talking throughout the ordeal, bore the large initials 'RL' at the front of his shirt and spoke with a Barbadian accent. He took the car key from the ignition and said, *"I got the keys so wunna can't run, and if wunna run, I gine burn the car."*

What followed was a period of inexplicable, weird and humiliating back-and-forth exchanges between Gunman R and the couple that seemed to go on forever.

Gesticulating with his small, silver gun, Gunman R said, *"I just want de money. Gimme de money."*

"Alright, we gine give you everything," Ian said nervously while trying to show a brave front. Ian, who was on the right side of the back seat, then moved as though to reach for his wallet.

"Sit down!" Gunman R shouted suddenly. *"Let the woman give me the money!"*

Wanda was so scared that she forgot she had left her bag at home, and for a few seconds searched the floor in front of her before she remembered. She then reached across between the front seats to the driver's door pocket where Ian kept his wallet and retrieved a brown bifold zipper wallet. Unzipping it, she handed Gunman R $55.00 comprised of two $20.00 notes, one $10.00 note and one $5.00 note.

Gunman R temporarily placed his torchlight in his left pants pocket. He took the money and then retrieved the torchlight. While she was reaching for the wallet, she heard sounds of Ian moving behind her.

"Stop moving!" shouted Gunman R, again.

Ian stopped.

Gunman L said nothing at all, just tapped the window glass occasionally with a dark-coloured gun he was carrying, flashing his torchlight in the car periodically.

Gunman R then told Ian, *"Lay down in the seat!"* The vehicle was small and Ian found this order difficult to carry out.

"How I gine lay down in the seat and she there?" he asked?

The man repeated his order and Ian repeated his answer.

"I can't talk to you," Gunman R said. *"Let the woman come near me and you go round de other side."*

The couple switched places and Gunman R asked, *"Wunna got on jewellery?"* He then told Ian, *"Give me that watch and that chain."*

Ian took off his round-faced gold watch and a small flat-linked gold chain with long and short alternating links and handed them to the man. Wanda took off her silver jewellery comprising a bracelet, earrings, a watch and two rings, and reached over to hand them to Gunman R. He spotted the light upon them and asked, *"Anything in there is gold?"*

"I don't wear gold," she replied.

"Keep it," he said, *"I don't want it."*

Wanda just dropped the jewellery in the vehicle.

Then to their utter horror, Gunman R said, *"Man, tek off wunna clothes!"*

Totally humiliated, Wanda took off her clothes and Ian took off his pants.

Gunman R said, *"I want to hurry up and leff but wunna holding out on me. Wunna playing tricks on me."*

"Wunna have everything. We don't have no more money in the car," said Ian.

"Shut up man! Put you head through the window," shouted Gunman R."

Wanda tried to explain that the window was up, and Gunman R said, *"Alright then. Put your head between the seats."*

"She there. I can't put my head between the seats," said Ian.

"Get down on your hands and knees right there!"

"I can't do that," Ian responded.

Gunman R decided to up the ante and taunted Wanda, demanding that she engage in sexually explicit acts with herself.

Wanda started to cry harder and with tears streaming down her face, she told him that she could not.

This agitated him further. *"You in there with a big man. Don't tell me no lies!"* he said angrily. Gunman R became livid and started to kick the car. *"Wunna holding out pun me. Open that cubby hole!"* he shouted. Gunman L just stood there, still not saying a word.

Ian leaned forward to comply but Gunman R stopped him. *"Man turn on that light,"* he said.

Ian turned on the roof light and opened the glove compartment which contained a box of tissues. The man then returned his attention to Wanda with another sexually degrading request.

"I ain't see that (private parts) yet, ya know."

Suddenly Gunman R said, *"I ain't here to rape you. I don't want to rape you."*

Ian then said something and Gunman R seemed to notice Ian's cellphone in front of the gear shift for the first time. *"Give me that phone!"* he shouted. Ian reached for it and seemed to press a button. Gunman R became impatient and started kicking the car door and beating the top with his hands and repeated his demand.

Ian said, *"I was only reaching for my pants. I giving you the phone."* He reached forward and Gunman R took the phone and slammed it on the ground outside.

Ian put his pants on, and Gunman R said, *"Sit back down and keep quiet! Put your head between the seats."*

Ian started to say something, but Wanda urged him to obey. *"Ian, just sit down,"* she said.

"Yeah Ian, just do it," Gunman R told him. He then asked Ian, *"Wuh you does do?"*

Ian did not answer.

He asked him where he lived, and Ian responded by saying, *"You just call my name. That means you know me. You know me and I know you."*

Ian did not call a name, so his girlfriend did not know if he knew the man or not.

Gunman R then repeated his earlier statements: *"Wunna playing games with me"*.

He then took the wallet from the floor of the car.

"This is a different wallet or the same one wunna give me the money out of?"

"Same one," Ian replied.

The man took up the wallet, looked through it and said, *"Man I gine keep this ID cos you giving me a lot of talk,"* referring to Ian's Barbados identification card. He then dropped the wallet in the seat and said, *"I don't want to be here, yuh know. I feel wunna holding out on me."*

Using the key, Gunman R opened the trunk of the car, searched for a few seconds, shut the lid and came back to the driver's door.

She heard the sound of the key on the car. *"Put you head through this window,"* Gunman R said to Wanda, motioning with the gun in the direction she should move.

She complied.

Calmly, Gunman R placed the gun to the right side of her forehead and asked Ian, *"Man, I got everything?"*

"Yes," Ian replied.

"Cos I got six bullets in this gun," Gunman R continued. *"I would put three in you and three in she."*

He then asked her age and address and she answered him. She was crying throughout the entire ordeal and he said, incongruously, *"You safe. You safe,"* and shockingly knocked fists with her, as friends would do.

Turning to Ian he said, *"The only reason I ain't shoot you is because of she, ya know."*

There was a short silence, and Gunman R's attention seemed to be on his partner, Gunman L.

"Wunna don't move. I coming back now," Gunman R said.

Wanda then realised that Gunman L had moved away and was walking towards the roadway. As Gunman R moved to join him, she saw that he was wearing long blue jeans.

As soon as they left, Ian used the temporary distraction to put things in motion. He quickly pushed forward the left front seat and got out of the car. Gunman R suddenly looked around. *"I tell wunna don't move! Where you going? Get back in the car and sit down!"* he ordered.

Ian ignored him saying, *"I looking for the keys."* He walked around the car saying, *"Where the keys? Where the keys?"*

"Get back in the car!" bellowed Gunman R again.

Suddenly, in what many might consider an unwise move, Ian took up a rock and threw it at Gunman R. It is unclear whether it struck him or not, but the man ran a short distance and then threw a rock back in Ian's direction. It struck the car and Ian ran in the opposite direction as though going further into the darkness of the developing community.

Wanda, terrified that Ian was leaving her, went into panic mode and a deeper dread gripped her. Going into survival mode, she got out of the car naked and ran as fast as she could in the direction of the highway to the north. Just before she ran, she saw Ian run past the car in the direction of the two gunmen, but she continued running towards the highway.

That was the last time she saw Ian alive.

As she ran, Wanda started screaming, *"Help! Help!"* repeatedly.

Wanda heard the sound of a single gunshot in the distance behind her.

Meanwhile, around 12:50 a.m., Police Constable Wayne Stuart was on duty with other policemen travelling along a section of the ABC Highway. They were on patrol in a police car and because of a previous robbery in the area, had made a check around the area where Ian and Wanda had gone to park out. They were about to leave when they heard what they thought was a woman's voice screaming, *"Help! Help!"* coming from the right-side area of the road.

Almost immediately after, they heard an explosion similar to that of a gunshot and the policemen stopped the vehicle.

Wanda neared the highway and saw a parked white car. Naked and terrified out of her mind, and not knowing who was in the car, she ran towards it, desperate to flee from the gunmen who had held up her and her boyfriend. She could see that there were three men in the car but continued on towards them.

When they stopped, the policemen saw a naked woman coming from a bushy area, running in their direction. The woman was screaming, crying and hysterical. The three officers alighted the vehicle and identified themselves as police officers.

"Help me! I was robbed!" she cried.

The policemen tried to calm down the woman. They assured her that they were indeed police officers and that she was safe with them. They were placing her in the vehicle when two more loud explosions pierced the night. The sounds seemed to come from the area to the right of the road but closer to the entrance of Southern Heights Development.

One of the policemen left with the woman in the vehicle, leaving the other policemen behind. The two policemen then heard a fourth loud explosion, this time to the left side of the road. They went in the direction they had seen the young woman run from and came upon a parked motor car. The area was in complete darkness. The car was red and the front left and right doors were open. The right driver's door glass was shattered, and other minor damage could be seen. Looking inside, the interior appeared to have been searched.

The police officers started to search the area around the car when they received information about a second occupant of the car. They were now looking for a man – Ian Matthews – but could not find him. Soon after, several police officers converged on the scene.

Police Constable Allan Goodridge was one of the officers that responded. Hearing shouts coming from north of where they were, he and other sergeants drove back towards the area where they heard the voices.

Getting out of the vehicle, PC Goodridge moved towards a dark, bushy area. He used a torchlight to search the area and continued until he reached a sporting facility. There he met another police officer who identified himself. Seeing the light, more police officers came and met up with the two. Equipped with torchlights, the recently arrived officers followed the one who was already at the scene.

Ian is found barely alive

The police continued to search the area and after about half an hour, the body of a man was found lying on his left side in the centre of the sporting facility, between two trees. One of the police officers lifted the man's head into his lap. PC Goodridge instructed that policeman to keep talking to the man to keep him alert but the man was unresponsive to touch and sound and was in and out of consciousness. Groans were all that escaped his lips.

PC Goodridge then shone his light on the man's body and noticed a wound in the lower section of his abdomen.

By then, Ian had stopped groaning. PC Goodridge made a further check and realised that he was still breathing. Realising this, the policemen on the scene didn't wait for an ambulance but lifted the wounded man into a police vehicle where he was transported to the Accident and Emergency Department of the Queen Elizabeth Hospital for further medical treatment.

A team of doctors tried to resuscitate the man but were unsuccessful. Ian Matthews was pronounced dead shortly after arriving at the hospital.

The police returned to secure the scene around the car and immediately commenced their investigations.

A comprehensive search was made of the scene with the assistance of personnel from other units of the Royal Barbados Police Force and one canine unit.

A Flex Tuff brand glove was found on the roadway and taken into evidence.

Shoe impressions were found in a sandpit and these were cast by one of the Sergeants and preserved.

A cap and a mask were soon found: the cap in a bushy area to the west of the parkout spot, the mask on the left side of the road when facing the ABC Highway.

Ian Matthews' car – exterior view from passenger's side

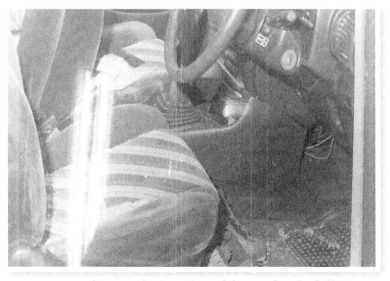

Damage done to the interior of the car by the killers

A report by a nearby resident indicated that he had seen a man running through the development area. His description of the runner closely matched the details Wanda had given previously. This led police to conclude that the perpetrators had used the sporting facility to make their escape.

Wanda had been taken to a nearby police station by the police officer where she reported the incident. She stated that to the best of her knowledge, Ian did not have a gun on that night.

She gave a full account to the police of what happened during the night of terror which included some details about the assailants' builds, their clothes and what they were doing: *They were both of slim build and appeared to be in their early 20s; Gunman R was about 6 feet tall, wore gloves and greyish coloured full-face ski mask; Gunman L was about 5 feet 9 inches tall, wore dark, oval-shaped sunglasses with gold frames, the glasses narrowed towards the side; wore neither a mask nor gloves and he never spoke throughout the ordeal. The incident took about thirty minutes and Ian resisted throughout.*

Police investigations

House-to-house enquiries were conducted in the areas surrounding the murder scene. Persons were interviewed but nothing was gleaned which could assist in any significant way. The roadblocks set up in the area and interviewing of persons passing in vehicles derived no measures of success.

With little actionable intelligence from the area canvass, the investigations then focused on persons known for committing robberies and other firearm offences since it seemed clear, from Wanda's account, that the primary objective was to rob the occupants of the vehicle at the time. Ian's death, police surmised, most likely resulted from his bold confronting of the assailants.

One woman would report later that while she was outside liming with a friend, she went to buy some cocaine and this guy came up to them and asked if they heard gunshots and she said, *"No."* She told police, however, that she had heard one explosion which sounded very faint and she thought it was a bomb.

Lovers' Lane Robberies

Common Features of Lovers' Lane Robberies

- breaking the driver's window with a stone

- spotting torchlights in victims' eyes for a blinding and disorienting effect

- demanding money and gold jewellery

- females ordered to search for jewellery

- culprits searching the boot of the car

- leaving the victims in the boot of the car

'*Lovers' Lane Robberies*' had been adopted by the police as the common name for a spate of robberies that had taken place over a few months. All of the crimes occurred in areas where amorous couples had gone for romantic adventures. The assailants would rob the couples, force them to remove their clothing, and demand the women engage in sexually demeaning acts.

The case of Ian and Wanda was added to the list.

Police determined that the cases were all linked as the behaviours exhibited by the two culprits were remarkably consistent throughout the series of criminal activities.

In all cases, at least one individual is armed with a gun and this individual would threaten to shoot if the demands were not met. In most cases, he took command intending to suppress resistance from any male victim. These robbers preferred gold jewellery with cash. If the jewellery did not appear to be gold or of sufficient quality, or silver, it was refused.

Persons were interviewed that were considered possible suspects but nothing useful was obtained to connect any of them to the crime.

The word on the street was that two men who roamed the streets of Silver Hill were responsible for the crime. One of them was picked up and found with a 9 mm gun in his possession. The gun was checked, but it did not match the firearm used in the murder of Ian Matthews, since the bullet recovered from Ian's body was fired from a .32 revolver.

Wanda told the police that the men were armed, and the two men picked up were always armed. One of them was charged in connection with a firearm found in his possession and was remanded in custody. During his interview, he maintained that he was not involved in Ian Matthews' murder.

Six of the fourteen persons who were interviewed during the initial investigations were later incarcerated for other crimes.

The glove which was found near the scene was shown to several persons to have it identified but no one had seen such a glove before.

Despite intensive investigations, nothing came up to assist in solving the crime.

A photograph taken on the fatal night of the deceased wearing a flat-linked gold chain was scanned for enhancement, but was still not visible enough to make copies. Police contacted Wanda to determine if a satisfactorily clear photograph of Ian wearing the gold chain could be found, but she had none.

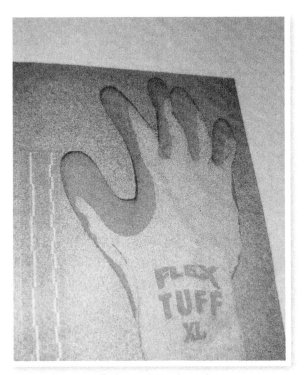

Picture of glove found at the scene

As the investigations into the murder continued, the police located a company in Barbados which imported the Flex Tuff brand of gloves for their production staff. A staff list was acquired from the company and was profiled. It was discovered that the gloves were imported by the company from as early as 2000. Any suspicion of possible staff involvement in the crime was dismissed as none of the names on the staff could be linked to the crime.

Six months after the murder, several search warrants were executed in the hope of finding the .32 revolver, which would assist in solving the crime.

The searches turned up nothing.

Did Ian Matthews know one of his assailants or was that just a tactic to offset Gunman R? Did he sacrifice himself to save Wanda? Might he have lived were he not so determined to resist his armed adversaries?

We may never know.

Robberies, rapes, sexual humiliation and physical abuse have all been perpetrated by criminals against their victims at various *lovers' lane* spots across Barbados. While little good can come of a murder, it seems the murder of Ian Matthews had one positive outcome: the number of Barbadians who are prepared to risk outdoor romance in their cars appears to have significantly reduced.

Have lovers in Barbados truly learnt their lessons?

Only time will tell.

CHAPTER SIX

Dead Men Tell No Tales

"No, no, Lord, no, no!"

Oneata thought she recognised the voice that carried to her window from not far away. Ordinarily, she might have called out or gone out to check.

But the last few seconds were anything but ordinary. Two loud explosions had just shattered the quiet night of the Kirtons, St. Philip community on Saturday, July 17th, 2004.

Oneata knew the explosions were gunshots. She also believed the distressed voice to be that of her neighbour and good friend, Greg. Oneata and Greg had known each other for the past nine years.

Eleven-year-old Kymani also heard the loud explosions and immediately became worried. His father recently left home to walk to the Texaco Star Mart at Kirtons for a snack. Though it was late in the night, this was the norm for his dad, who would usually return home soon. But the gunshots – and that is what Kymani thought they were – bothered him, so he went to his mother's bedroom and woke her, telling her that something was wrong with his father; that he had gone to the gas station and not returned yet, and that he had heard gunshots shortly after his father had left home.

Very troubled, Kymani called his dad's cell phone. No answer.

"He said something had to be wrong with his father because he was taking too long to come home and he had heard a gunshot," his mother, Regina, reported to police later.

Regina, too, tried reaching Greg, but he did not answer. Returning to bed, she told Kymani that she did not get through. Changing her mind, she told her son that she would go and check to see if Greg was at the potential shooting. She was putting on her clothes to go outside when the telephone rang. She answered and it was her mother, asking if she had heard of a shooting up by her. She told her mother no, she did not hear anything but Kymani had told her about hearing gunshots. She also explained to her mother that Kymani had also told her that Greg had gone up the road.

Regina's mother then told her that someone had called her asking what her (Regina's) husband's last name was.

Regina then heard her sister's voice in the background. She had just reached their mother's home. Hearing that Regina was on the phone, her sister said she was coming right over.

While waiting for her sister to arrive, Regina checked her telephone. There were two missed calls: the caller ID showed one number while the other was private, name and number withheld.

Regina would learn subsequently that the unknown name and number belonged to her neighbour, Oneata. Still concerned, she called the Shepherd's residence hoping to hear Greg and enquire if he had heard the explosions. There was no reply at that time from the telephone.

Receiving a tip from an anonymous person walking the road about 10.55 p.m. that night, officers at District C Police Station were mobilised and soon found a motionless body lying on the roadway.

Barbadians are known to flock to bloody scenes. As Regina looked outside, people were already heading up the street and she was told someone had been shot.

It was only after she got her worried son to sleep that Regina headed to the scene. Her son had tried to reach his father on his cellphone earlier but received no response. Regina had tried as well and also failed to get an answer. Other family members tried. Nothing.

At the scene, the hubbub of the gathering crowd was broken intermittently by the many trills of a cellphone on the lifeless body.

Greg would never answer that cell again.

In the wee hours of the morning, with her brother, sister, her husband's sister and a cousin there, Regina confirmed that it was her husband who had been shot.

If you were arguing that all murders are senseless and far beyond the pale, then the killing of Greg Shepherd would be your reference case.

Greg, 36 years old, was the first of six children born to Joan Shepherd. A quiet unassuming young man who generally kept to himself, he was employed as an insurance agent with an Insurance Company at the time of his death.

Greg was an avid steel pannist and organised the Four Roads Primary School Steel Band. Married to Regina for four years, the two were the parents of 11-year-old son, Kymani. The couple however, was estranged.

On the morning of July 17th, 2004, Regina left home to do the supermarket run leaving Greg and Kymani at home.

There was a steel pan festival at Weiser's Bar on Spring Garden that afternoon and Greg had booked the school band to play. At about 1:00 p.m., Greg left home with Kymani, dropped him off at his grandmother's residence, and headed to Weiser's where he performed with the school band.

Greg returned home about 10:30 p.m. that night, parked his car in the garage and went inside. Kymani was still up and playing a game on the television. Regina was asleep in her bedroom.

Feeling peckish, Greg decided he would head to the Star Mart for a snack. He changed his shoes and left the house.

He was shot and killed minutes later.

His death shocked the community of Kirtons in St Philip.

Road where Greg Shepherd was gunned down

A post-mortem revealed that death was caused by one gunshot, the bullet entering the back and exiting the front of the abdomen.

With Greg's wallet and jewellery still on his body after he was killed, police initially ruled out the motive of robbery.

With no eyewitnesses coming forward and little forensic evidence of note at the scene, police investigations were severely hampered. They worked the case from all angles but leads were few and revealed little. The case soon went cold and remained cold for five years.

Breakthrough?

A potential major breakthrough in the case came in 2009, when, based on investigations from the Major crimes unit police interviewed a man named Kirk from St Philip. The information arising from the interview led police to arrest him under suspicion of murdering Greg.

Kirk stated that two men had asked him to drive and take them to Packers in Christ Church to collect a gun.

"I was driving and Don get out in Kirtons and shoot that man just foolish so," he said.

When the police asked him who these persons were, he said Don and Nolan.

"All two of them get kill after that. The police shoot Nolan and Don get murdered," said Kirk.

When asked why he did not report the matter to the police after the men had died, he said, *"Because dead men can't get charge, I would end up getting charged and I don't want to spend 15 years in prison for something I ain't do."*

This is Kirk's statement:

"A few years ago, sometime during the night I was at home eating some food. My grandfather was still alive and was also at the house. As I was about to put my plate in the kitchen sink, I heard my friends Don and Nolan outside shouting for me. I went to them and Nolan told me that he wanted me to borrow my grandfather's car to take himself and Don some place. I asked him where they wanted to go, and they said that they wanted me to take them to Packers to collect a gun. He did not say from whom they were going to collect the gun.

I was accustomed giving them drops to do miscellaneous things. I told him that I will take them but not in my grandfather's car which was a taxi. Nolan offered to pay me money to get my grandfather's car but I told him that I did not want his money. They started to walk away, couple minutes to put on a shirt. About 20 minutes later, Nolan, Don and

I left my house and walked to (a specific area) in St Philip. We went to a road which took you to a children's playpark and I saw a silver grey Lantis parked on the road by the fence to the play park facing out.

Nolan had the key to this car and gave it to me. I got in the driver's seat. Nolan got on the front passenger seat and Don sat in the back seat behind Nolan. I drove from there to Packers. Nolan directed me to a dead end road at Packers and he told me to stop. Both of them got out of the car and said that they would be coming back now.

They walked through a track and disappeared. I waited in the car and did not see exactly where they went. They both returned about 25 minutes later and sat down in the car as they had been sitting before. I saw that Don was in the back seat and he was fiddling with a black automatic gun.

I drove off and Don passed the gun forward to Nolan who looked at it and fiddled with it. He said that he was checking to see if the gun was working good. They did not talk about doing anything specific with the gun.

I drove along the same route we had come and when I reached Kirton's junction and was slowing down at the major stop, Don told me to stop. I stopped about 4 or 5 feet from the stop sign and was wondering why he told me to stop just so.

Don got out of the car and I saw that a man was walking past the car going to the direction of Mangrove. Don jogged across to the side of the road where the man was walking. He went and stood in front of him, pointed the gun at the man and told him to pass everything. The man put his hands in the air and screamed. He turned as if he was going to run, and I heard a loud explosion and saw the man drop to the ground. He then sat up and was still screaming.

Don ran back to the car, jumped in the back seat and told me to drive. I drove off and they directed me to park the car in the new area of St. Philip which was now being paved. Don was panicking and was telling me "Nolan, that is bare cunt" and that the gun just went off.

Don still had the gun and he placed his body in between the two front seats of the car. He looked at me and told me that if I mentioned or said anything to anybody, I know what would happen to me.

I was petrified and I did not sleep for weeks. I parked the car and left the keys in the ignition and told Nolan and Don that I would never go anywhere with them again and not to speak to me or come around me anymore. I cursed them and told Don that he did cunt and they started to laugh and said that I was freaking out.

I walked away and went home, leaving them. The next morning, I heard people saying that a man had died at Kirtons. Nolan and Don did not come around me, nor did I tell anyone about the shooting because I did not know who to trust and I have two boy children to look after. I did not want anything to happen to me or to the children."

Police interviewed an acquaintance of Kirk, who said that Kirk thought that Nolan and Don, as well as Don's brother, wanted to kill him because they thought he was the weak link in the group and might talk about what they had done. The acquaintance told police that this was the reason why Kirk left and went to England because the men broke into his house and stole his clothes. He said that they would also intimidate Kirk by shaping their hands in that of a gun and pointing at him when they passed by him. Why was Kirk not arrested and charged for the murder of Greg Shepherd? Was his statement not tantamount to a full confession? Even a "full confession" has to be verified and corroborated and in the absence of a statement from the other two men and with no other evidence, There was little for which he could have been charged.

Was it really a random killing?

Of all the persons on the street that night, why was Greg targeted?

The murder of Greg Shepherd remains unsolved.

CHAPTER SEVEN

Abducted!

Kidnapping is not a crime that is common in Barbados. In fact, the familiarity of Barbadians with kidnapping is more likely to be associated with movie scenes. The scene that unfolded on September 19th, 2005 could be described as one straight from an action-thriller Hollywood movie. Mark Swenson, aged 22 years, of a suburban community in St. Michael, was forcibly taken from his residence by four unknown men.

He never returned home.

Mark lived with his parents and attended a St. Michael's school. He did not succeed academically and never maintained a steady job after leaving school. Mark quickly got involved in the drug world, assisting in the transportation of drugs for a major drug lord named Shawn from a neighbouring community.

Soon after starting the relationship with Shawn, he began keeping large quantities of marijuana at his parents' home for Shawn and became known in the drug world as "Shawn's Stashman." Mark was always in the company of Shawn and would be seen from time to time driving Shawn's SUV.

A tempestuous and abusive relationship

Mark liked the girls and the girls liked Mark. Patricia, however, was considered his 'main girl'. Mark met her while partying in a nightclub in Barbados called 'Le Club' and they quickly became lovers. From all accounts, his relationship with Patricia was an abusive one. They would see each other on and off because, according to her, Mark was involved with a lot of younger women.

"He would tell me that I cannot finish with him and would beat me and threaten to kill me," Patricia told police after he went missing, *"...and I would always forgive him."*

"One day he came to my apartment and broke a glass window," she recalled. As a result of the incident at her apartment, her landlord told her she had to leave. She also said that Mark would come to her workplace and threaten to kill her.

During their relationship, she saw Mark with a gun on one occasion. She was in the kitchen cooking and Mark was outside her house working on his car. Her young son, who was in the living room watching television, went unusually quiet. Curious, she left the kitchen to check on him and to her utter amazement, her son was sitting on the floor playing with a small silver gun!

Mark came in from outside and picked up the gun. She never saw the gun again. When she queried about the whereabouts of the gun, Mark told her that he gave the gun to one of his friends. The police came on the block one day and the friend threw it away.

"I was afraid of him at the time. He was on drugs and could not go to sleep unless he smoked."

Patricia told police that Mark would beat her in public spaces as well. Due to his violent outbursts and embarrassing behaviour, she stopped partying at the club.

She had started partying at another club – Club Extreme – and Mark found out and began stalking her.

"Mark would follow me all about the place. He was jealous and never liked me to talk to any person. One night he found me in Club Extreme and dragged me outside and beat me up, swelling up my face, bruising and scarring me".

The abusive relationship with Mark even played out in front of Patricia's son. *"At one point, he even beat me up in front of my son, who was just a toddler at the time."*

Tired of the abuse in all forms, Patricia stayed away from him for about a month. She said that his mother, who was fond of her, and who would always intervene in their relationship, invited her over to her house for a function. Even though she and Mark were not on speaking terms, she accepted the invitation.

Mark was not at the function but came home when it was over. They talked to each other, and he started to cry, asking her to forgive him. His mother also talked to her and asked her to forgive Mark and according to Patricia, *"...tried to soften my heart."*

He then asked her to spend the night with him, and she agreed.

"We started to make love, and then he wanted sex. I told him that I was not in for it. He accused me of sleeping around and said that maybe I am not 'tight' anymore and that I was having sex with other men."

Raped and lit on fire

"He tore off my panty, then forced me to have sex with him. He told me that in order for me to get away from him, I would have to get a drug lord to kill him fast."

After he forced Patricia to have sex with him, he went on to the patio and smoked a marijuana *spliff*. He later returned to the bedroom with a bottle of rubbing alcohol while she was sitting on the bed.

Suddenly, Patricia's worst nightmare occurred. Mark then began throwing the alcohol in her face and over her body!

"I closed my eyes and stood up and placed my hands on the bedroom wall for support. I then fell to the ground. Mark then flicked a lighter he had in his hand and I heard "buff!" and I caught ablaze! He then started to beat me up with a pillow."

Patricia managed to get off her burning shirt and ran down the corridor of the house, shrieking, still burning, and into the bathroom. She turned on the water, still screaming as the pain of her melting skin was beyond bearing.

All the commotion caught the attention of Mark's mother, who ran out of her bedroom to see what was the matter.

Mark looked at his mother and selfishly and without any remorse said:

"If you take her to the hospital, the police will come for me. Can you deal with that?"

Looking at him, she sighed.

Then Mark's mother called a private doctor.

The doctor arrived but indicated that Patricia was severely burnt and needed hospitalisation. They then wrapped her in a wet towel and took her to the Queen Elizabeth Hospital. She remained there for two days before being transferred to Bayview Hospital where she stayed for over six weeks. For whatever reason, the police were never called in connection with Mark's actions.

The abuse starts again

While Patricia was in the hospital, Mark visited her. Once again, she forgave him and decided to recuperate at his home.

Three days after she left the hospital, still badly burnt and unable to do anything for herself, Mark beat her again.

Patricia decided that she had to leave. She waited until he fell asleep, took up his van and drove it away to her mother's house.

Seeing Patricia's condition, her mother encouraged her to report the entire matter to the police – from the burning to the most recent beating.

Mark was taken into custody and charged by the police. He was sent to the Psychiatric Hospital for three weeks to undergo evaluation. During that time, his mother told Patricia that he wanted to see her, and she eventually visited the Psychiatric Hospital to see him.

After he was released from hospital, Mark was admitted to Verdun House, a drug rehabilitation facility, where he stayed for nine months. When Mark was discharged from Verdun House, he and Patricia reconciled their differences and rekindled their relationship.

But Mark had not changed.

From all accounts, he was aggressive by nature. Patricia recalled an incident at a nightclub in St James when Mark tried to trouble her several times while she was partying with some friend of hers. That night, he stabbed a male friend of hers several times, but his motive was not stated by Patricia.

She decided to leave the nightclub because she feared that he would embarrass her. Many nights she opted not to go out because she did not want him to turn up and embarrass her at the club.

Fight in Le Club nightclub

Two weeks before Mark's abduction, on September 19th, 2005, Patricia and some of her friends visited Le Club around 3:00 a.m. and saw Mark in the club, dancing. Also at the club were two men from the Eden Lodge and Cave Hill communities Things between the two men and Mark became heated, a fight broke out. The security promptly ejected all three men from the club.

Once outside, the fracas escalated and soon bottles and stones were whizzing back and forth. Eventually, the fight was broken up by other patrons.

At the time, Patricia and Mark were not on good terms. She had rented a car about a week prior and the two argued because he wanted to borrow the car, but she refused to lend it to him.

She had her reasons.

A few weeks earlier he had told her that some weed was coming in for Shawn and the drug landing was taking place that same week. Unrelated to this information, Patricia rented a car the next week and one night she and two of her friends went to McBrides in St. Lawrence Gap. That night, Mark told her that he wanted the car because he had to clear some weed. She allowed him to use the car and after he dropped them off at McBrides, Mark left with the car. He never came back for them, and they were forced to resort to taking a taxi home, much to their annoyance.

The next day when Mark returned the car it smelled strong of marijuana. Patricia was angry and told him about the scent.

"I tell you that the weed landing and I had to do what I had to do, so why you vex?" he said to her.

Drug landing

Police investigations revealed that on September 4th, 2005, a shipment containing one thousand, one hundred pounds (1,100lbs) of marijuana from St Vincent and consigned to Shawn, landed at an undisclosed location in the north of the island. One thousand pounds was for Shawn and one hundred pounds was for Lincoln, another drug dealer, who controlled a block called 'The Green Devils Block'.

Days before the drugs landed, Shawn had contracted Lincoln to assist in moving the drugs from the boat at sea when it arrived. This was done because Lincoln's group – known as the 'Back Alley Block' – were exceptionally good swimmers. On the night of the landing, Mark drove the vehicle in which Shawn travelled and was referred to by the Back Alley Block as the Transporter.

After clearing the drugs, Lincoln expected fifty pounds of marijuana as payment for his part in the operation. However, when the bale was weighed, it was found to be half a pound short. Arrangements were made between Shawn and Lincoln to collect the shortage on the following day. As planned, Lincoln collected the outstanding poundage the following day. Lincoln again took members of his group with him to collect the drugs.

On September 17th, 2005, Mark rented a green Toyota Sprinter motor car. His mother made the arrangements for him, and the car was to be returned on the 19th.

As arranged, the owner called Mark's home on the morning of the 19th to make the necessary arrangements to collect the car. A female answered the telephone and requested the car for an additional four days. The owner agreed and about 7:00 p.m. Mark met him on the outside of his home and paid the cost of the rental.

The day he was abducted

On September 19th, 2005, Mark telephoned Patricia and told her to come by his house. She refused. The two had an argument on the phone and she did not see or hear Mark for the remainder of the day which she found strange as he normally called her often. She stayed at home with one of her girlfriends who visited her.

After Patricia declined his offer to come by his house, Mark then called another female friend, Shantelle, on her cell phone and explained to her that he was in a fight in Le Club two weeks prior, which had left him sore and asked her to come over to give him a massage. Shantelle agreed to this, and Mark collected her and headed to Shawn's residence to transport him and his friends to Holetown.

As they passed Queen's College School, Mark started to blow the car horn continuously at a white car that was ahead of them until the driver stopped. A dark man with a chubby face and his hair plaited in a cornrow style then looked through his window and told Mark that the fellows that he fought in Le Club had said, *"It ain't done there."*

Curious, Shantelle asked Mark who this person was, and Mark said, *"He's another boss from another block."* They continued to drive along the same road and headed in the direction towards the main road and onto Cave Hill. As they passed a pasture on the left by a pavilion, Mark rolled up his window and told her that the man he got into a fight with lived in the area.

They continued on, collected Shawn and drove around with him all day, dropping him back to his residence later that evening.

Shantelle would later recount to police that the white car followed them the entire day, driving awfully close up to the rear of their car but Mark did not seem to be bothered.

During the early part of the night, Mark used the vehicle to transport drugs and to collect money owed to Shawn for drugs from persons in the north of the island. He was accompanied by Shantelle and a male friend who lived in his neighbourhood.

After completing these duties, Mark took Shantelle and the other friend to a neighbouring community, spent some time there and then the three headed back to his home. Mark dropped off his friend in the neighbourhood.

At home, Mark asked Shantelle if she was hungry and she said yes. They decided they would pick up something to eat from a nearby Chefette restaurant and set out. While at the drive-thru, Shantelle saw the white car following them again driving in the same manner as before, but this time with bright lights on. She again asked Mark why the car was behind them, and he said he did not know. As it was nighttime, they could not see who was driving the car, but once again Mark did not appear to be concerned about the car.

Heading back to Mark's home, they saw the white car tailing them again, tucked in close behind, bright lights blazing. This continued until Mark neared his home. The white car turned off into a gap and Mark and Shantelle headed inside.

While in his bedroom, Mark told her that he was going to the living room to tell his father about the fight that happened in the club and left the bedroom for a brief period. Shortly afterwards, he rejoined Shantelle in the bedroom.

Around 9:10 p.m., Mark was still in his bedroom with Shantelle when his father came to the room and informed him that someone was outside calling him. Mark got up, went to a wrought iron door in his parents' room and answered the caller. He told the caller that he did not know him and asked him to come into the light. The person, who was in a white shirt, said he was someone's cousin. Mark told him that he did not know that *"someone"* either. The person then walked away and went towards a white car which was parked on the roadway a little distance from the house on the southern side.

Mark's father opened the door and he, Mark and Mark's mother went out on the patio.

The white car was still parked in the roadway. They all went back inside.

Mark then went to the main door of the house and looked through the louvres. His father asked him if the car had gone, and he said it was still outside.

The man in the white shirt then came back to the house and approached the gate leading to the house and told Mark to come outside. Mark declined and instead invited the person into the patio where he turned on the electric lights. The caller then asked him where the dogs were, and Mark told him to come, that the dogs were secured.

The man walked into the patio with his head bowed, moved to the right-side louvre panel where Mark was and whispered something to him.

Mark then opened the door and went outside to the man. This could have been the mistake that cost him his life.

Mark and the man then walked towards the gate and appeared to be talking. His parents, becoming concerned, followed Mark outside. As he walked with the man towards the gate, he told his parents that everything was alright and to go back inside. His parents complied.

As soon as Mark exited the gate, three men got out of the car, grabbed Mark and started pulling him towards the car.

"Mummy and Daddy come!" Mark screamed.

Mark's parents quickly spun around and saw him struggling with three men who had him constrained in a tight grip and were trying to force him into the white car.

Both parents went quickly to help their son. The father valiantly tried to pull Mark away from the assailants but was unsuccessful. Mark, now desperate, grabbed his father while the men tried to put him in the car. Mark pulled his father towards him, telling his father to come with him and see where the men were taking him.

The oldest looking of the assailants remained outside the car, held Mark's mother by her hand and told her, *"Mums, you don't know what your son is up to. He took our stuff and then spend the money on this,"* and pointed to the car which Mark had rented.

He also told her he wanted to go into the house to search. She refused and told him she was going to call the police.

Apart from struggling with the men trying to get Mark into the car, Mark's parents never raised the alarm during the ordeal.

The men warned Mark's father to move back and stay away. The older man issued instructions: *"Put him in the car."* Then one of the men holding Mark took an unidentified object and struck him in the head. Stunned, Mark released his grip on his father. Later, police learned that Mark's father also had a bruised forehead but was unable to say how he got the injury.

Mark was shoved into the car and retained by two of the assailants. The others quickly bundled in, and the car sped off.

Meanwhile, at the Swenson residence, Mark's father returned inside where he saw Shantelle in the living room talking to his wife. Shantelle had Mark's cell phone and his mother told her to call the police. She said she was trying but was not getting through. She then called a number on the phone and spoke with Shawn.

Shawn listened attentively to what he was being told and responded by going to Mark's residence in his SUV accompanied by a man named Junior. He was told which way Mark had been whisked off and headed off in that direction. Shawn saw the brake lights of a vehicle outside Mark's home and accelerated towards it. The driver of the vehicle gunned the engine and sped away. Shawn tried to follow but could not catch up with it.

He came back about five minutes later and said that he lost the car. He briefly stood outside the house and then left.

Mark's father then telephoned the police and reported the matter. At that time, Shantelle told the Swensons that the white car had been following them all day. She then said that she was leaving. With that, Shantelle got into the hired car and left, saying that she would return but never did. She also took Mark's phone with her.

The police subsequently responded, searched the area and interviewed the persons who were at Mark's house when the abduction occurred, including Shantelle who they subsequently traced.

Around 11:00 p.m. that night, Mark's mother received a call on her cell phone from an unknown number. The voice, which she recognised as Mark, said, "*Mummy...*" and was cut off abruptly.

About five minutes later, the telephone rang again. The person on the phone said he was Mark and indicated that he did not know where he was. His mother would report subsequently that he was crying but had said the men had not harmed him and would bring him back home. "*The men said do not call the police and they will release me,*" Mark told his mother, and she could hear voices in the background saying not to call the police. She told Mark that she had already called the police and he said, "*Alright,*" and the call ended.

They never heard from him again.

John, a friend of Mark and another of Shawn's associates who delivered drugs for him, was at home the same night Mark was abducted. It was around 11:00 p.m. when he heard his telephone ringing. He answered.

It was Mark on the phone. Mark told him that he was being held by four "Vincy" (Vincentian) men and...

Abruptly, a man with a Barbadian accent came on the phone and said, *"If you want your man, you got to deliver two hundred pounds of weed,"* and ended the conversation. John was also in possession of one of Shawn's phones at the time and a call soon came through on it, repeating the request, but this time for one hundred and fifty pounds of marijuana. John told the caller that he was not Shawn and the caller then asked him if he was the driver of the blue van, referring to the van that was used to transport drugs.

John said yes and the caller said, *"You are the transporter, you know where the weed is, and if you do not hand over the weed, we will shoot you in your belly and shoot up the block."* Once again, the call ended abruptly.

Mark's girlfriend tries to reach him

Meanwhile, earlier in the night, about ten o'clock, Mark's girlfriend Patricia was toying with the idea of calling him, but her friend told her to go to sleep and forget him. She went to sleep but around 3:00 a.m. she woke up and sent him a text. There was no reply. She sent him another text and once again there was no reply. She then called his house phone about 5:00 a.m. and his sister Lori, answered the phone. Without identifying herself, she asked to speak to Mark, and his sister said he was not at home.

She then called Mark's cell phone and Shantelle, whom Patricia did not know at the time, answered the phone. She asked to speak to Mark and Shantelle said he was not there. She then asked Shantelle who she was and how she got Mark's cell phone and Shantelle hung up.

She again dialled the Swensons' home number and Lori answered. This time Patricia identified herself and asked if Mark was at home.

"Didn't you hear what happened?" asked Lori. *"No, what happened?"* asked Patricia. Lori then told her that four men had come to the house and kidnapped Mark.

She put down the phone, stunned.

Patricia then decided to take her friend home and then drove over to Mark's house, where she stayed for some time, waiting for positive news to come out of Mark's kidnapping.

Unfortunately, her wait was in vain: Mark never came home.

Eventually, Patricia returned home.

Sometime later, Patricia returned to the Swenson's home and spoke with the family. Stating that she had no idea who would abduct him, Patricia called Mark's friends, including Shawn, to see if they had heard anything, but nothing further had turned up.

On Sunday, September 25th, around 9:40 a.m., the phone rang at Mark's house. Patricia was there and she answered the call. A male voice was on the line and the person said they wanted to speak with the Swensons. She told the man that they were unavailable. The man then proceeded to ask who he was speaking to, and Patricia identified herself. He asked if she was the kidnapped boy's girlfriend? She said she was.

The man then said that he knew the whereabouts of the boy and if the family wanted to get him back, he would need some money. *"No problem"*, Patricia indicated. The man continued, saying that the boy was being held in a house and the men who had him would leave in the day and come back at night. He said the men had guns and, *"he does not get involved in nothing like that,"* but he would have to take somebody who also had a gun to back him up if something happened.

He then said he needed some money and asked how much she had. She asked how much he wanted, and he said between $4,000 - $5,000.00 and again she told him it was not a problem. He asked if she could meet him at Less Frills with the money and she told him that she had to go to the ATM in Bridgetown to get the money and to give her half an hour.

The man got aggressive, complaining that he just left Bridgetown and had to drive all the way up there. Patricia revised her time frame and told him to give her twenty minutes and she would make the exchange. He then told her he wanted Bds$2,000.00 and she agreed.

Patricia relayed this information and the whereabouts of the rendez-vous point to some of Mark's friends. They met up with the man – not Patricia – and beat him up.

He did not know where Mark was. He was only interested in black-mailing Mark's family.

Canefield where Mark Swenson's remains were found

The skull of Mark Swenson

On March 31st, 2006, six months after Mark's abduction, human skeletal remains were discovered in a partially harvested cane field in Christ Church.

Other items were found close to the remains. The items were secured by the police as it was suspected that they could have been Mark's.

The items – excluding the skeletal remains and other tangible physical evidence – were shown to the members of Mark's family who positively recognised them as belonging to Mark.

On April 6th, 2006, a postmortem examination on the remains was done by Dr. Stephen Jones at the Queen Elizabeth Hospital. It was determined that death was attributed to a gunshot head injury and other traumatic head injuries.

Forensic odontologist Dr. Victor Eastmond, conducted an odonatolog-ical examination using Mark's antemortem dental records. The examination showed conclusively that the remains were those of Mark Swenson.

Over 150 persons were interviewed concerning Mark's abduction and murder and statements taken from 40 of them. The police concluded that Mark's death was clearly linked to his involvement in the drug trade and his close association with Shawn. They also believed that there was some connection between his death and the drug landing on September 4th, 2005.

Though the police have not ruled out a foreign connection in this matter, the Back Alley Gang was suspected to be responsible for the kidnap-ping and murder of Mark Swenson. The leader of the gang, Christopher, severed ties and pulled away from the group, taking with him the major drug players in the gang.

Despite all of the hearsay that swirled about alleged hits and retribution by the Back Alley Gang, to date, no one has been charged with Mark's murder.

It is highly likely that no one ever will.

CHAPTER EIGHT

The Tragic End of a Beauty

No matter how young a person begins to abuse substances and/or their bodies, no one starts life as an addict or a prostitute. Somewhere along the line – and psychologists tend to favour early developmental stages – the confluence of circumstances, events and traumatic experiences seems to divert the individual down darker paths.

Sherene Gooding was a beautiful woman; some will argue stunning. Not too tall, not too short, Sherene was five feet five inches tall, bowlegged, with hazel eyes, a dainty nose and sporting a low haircut. One of her close associates described her as friendly, intelligent, and strong-willed. Another described her as being very direct: saying what she had to, regardless of how it impacted others. Yet another person described Sherene as someone who could represent herself, even if it came to blows.

From an early age, Sherene developed a love for hospitality and cosmetology, which helped her to excel in her restaurant job as well as at modelling. She also put her talents to use by assisting hair salons with makeup and pedicure and manicure applications. From all indications, she showed considerable potential to develop a successful career in cosmetology or modelling or both.

This early knowledge acquired on the job, allowed Sherene to transcend the usual social barriers. Always well-groomed, she had the ability to fit easily into conversations with people of different social classes and walks of life.

Sherene's family emigrated to the USA. There was clear evidence of a breakdown in the relationship, within her mother's family with whom she resided at the time. She moved in with her aunt but this was short-lived, and she soon left to room with friends while still in her teens.

The estranged family relationship would have an impact on Sherene as in subsequent years she would seek companionship from people she met, trying to develop the bonds that were missing from her family.

Sherene never got married but was involved in many intimate relationships which produced four children, all from different fathers.

Life changes

Sherene's promising career in hospitality changed dramatically when she was introduced to cocaine by the father of her first child, Genesis. For a time, she was able to maintain this vice without losing the handle on her life completely, but following her split from him, Sherene began to use a far more addictive form of cocaine – street name: *crack*.

A *high* from crack is usually more intense and lasts for a shorter time than the usual powdered cocaine. This quick dissipating but intense *high* of crack causes crack addicts to seek it more frequently and to the exclusion of accepted social behaviours. There was no 'keeping a handle' on her life this time and Sherene soon became unemployed. Work was no longer a priority. The next high was.

The craving drove her to seek refuge in Dover, Christ Church, a known drug haven with many drug *holes*. Here Sherene sought a place to live and source drugs but probably not in that order. Unable to support her drug habit financially, Sherene turned to prostitution to secure the funds to satisfy her cravings. Prostitution was soon an integral part of her life and she quickly gained notoriety with the nickname *Tarmac*.

Sherene received money from her mother and siblings who lived overseas and with these funds she was able to satisfy her demand for crack and alcohol. When she ran out of money, she would borrow money from persons she befriended. She repaid them with the money that she earned from prostitution and whatever she received from her mother and relatives and the cycle continued.

But even though Sherene had access to some money, it was always insufficient to support her addiction and so her life spiralled deeper and deeper into sexual promiscuity. It appeared that – she was prepared to exchange sex for money with any man who came along.

《《《 》》》

It was approaching the Holy Week of 2007 and everyone was preparing for Easter. The curtains in many Barbadian homes were being changed, the smell of pudding baking permeated the air, and children and the 'young at heart' were busy flying their kites.

It was a joyous time around the holidays.

On Monday, April 16th, 2007, one week after the Easter Monday bank holiday, two teenaged brothers, Chris and Rakeem were flying their kites in an open pasture west of 4th Avenue, Cane Vale, Christ Church – their neighbourhood – when one of the kites 'popped'. Like most young boys, they ran in search of the kite, keeping one eye on the kite's erratic descent and one eye on the uneven terrain beneath their feet.

Chris and Rakeem stumbled on a decomposed body.

The body was headless.

Terrified and traumatised, the two boys ran home to their grandfather who lived a stone's throw away to tell him of the grisly find.

The police were called and mobilised themselves immediately.

Location of the body of Sherene

They found the nude body and lying on its stomach with the hands tied to the rear. Present also were what seemed to be pieces of maggot-infested human abdomen. Investigations also disclosed that Sherene's cellphone was missing. The clothes which she was wearing when she was last seen was missing; jewellery which she usually wore was missing. It was surmised that Sherene could have been killed, according to medical evidence over a 4 to 5-day period.

A search revealed a black-handled knife near the body.

This raised the curtain on investigations that would set the police on a roller-coaster through a wild, yet sad story of despair, sex, drugs, rape, and murder.

The body was later identified by forensics as Sherene Blondina Gooding, a 38-year-old woman, whose last known address was Gall Hill, Christ Church.

At the time of her murder, Sherene lived with her boyfriend Derek Louis, but the "boyfriend" designation was in name only as the two lived separate lives: Sherene going her way, and Derek going his. She was a cocaine addict but also abused other drugs including alcohol. She also prostituted herself which led her to sleep at various residences. This was known and accepted by Derek, and it seemed he benefitted materially from Sherene's lifestyle.

Those close to Sherene knew that she often went for days without contacting anyone. For them, this was normal and so she was never reported missing.

The crime scene did not yield much to investigators. Police proffered the view that the place where the body was found was a *secondary* scene – in other words, the murder did not take place there, and Sherene's body was simply dumped at that location. According to forensic evidence, it was estimated that Sherene could have been killed four to five days before her body was found. Crucially, the primary scene was never identified.

Investigations also disclosed that Sherene's cellphone was missing. The clothes she was last seen wearing were also missing along with the jewellery she usually wore. The last time she was seen by her best friend Susan, she was wearing a long black skirt with two small splits on each side and two red stripes down the side, a black armhole blouse with a design covering the entire blouse, a pair of black slippers with a slight heel and carrying a small black knitted bag.

Police were stumped. What could have led the killer or killers to hack the head off Sherene's body? Was this to aid with the concealment of the crime or did this go beyond? Was it a crime of passion or was Sherene targeted? Was the decapitation a sign or symbol, and if so, to whom?

Police investigations identified two high-level suspects: Winston Shoman and Derek Matthews, but none of the information gathered had created a victim connection in recent times. There had been evidence to show that Sherene had access to finance and there was no time that she was seen carrying excess money, but there is an aspect of her demanding money from sexual acquaintances.

Investigators decided they would have to look more closely into Sherene's less recent past for anything that might help them to solve her murder. Information received by police suggested that all of Sherene's relationships had some element of domestic abuse and/or violence and so investigators continued to focus on past romantic interests. This led to rather interesting glimpses of Sherene's complicated world of sex and drugs.

William, a 71-year-old married man with adult children told police that Sherene would often ask him for a ride, and he would oblige and give her a ride in his motor van. Sherene sometimes visited his home in the company of his niece to drink and listen to music.

One day he received a telephone call from his niece who told him that Sherene said she liked him. He then told his niece to give Sherene his cell phone number. A few minutes later, he received a call from Sherene who told him she wanted to see him. He asked her why and she said she would give him the reason when she saw him. They arranged to meet a week later.

A week passed and Sherene went to see William. She asked him for money. He gave her $20.00 and she left. Later that day, Sherene returned to William's home along with his niece and the three sat together in the back, drinking alcohol.

When it was time for the two women to go, William got his van and the women bundled in and they set off. William dropped off his niece first and headed to where Sherene was living at the time. On route, Sherene told him to drive into a nearby churchyard and William, full of lust, complied. The two drove into the churchyard, parked and had sex in the back of William's van.

After the sex, Sherene told him that she did not want to pressure him, but she would normally charge $60.00 to $70.00 for the *services* she had just rendered. William was taken aback! He did not realise she wanted money in exchange for sex. He thought she was genuinely interested in him. He then drove her to Gall Hill, Christ Church and dropped her at the top of her gap.

William did not hear from Sherene for about a week, and he did not call her. Then, one evening while relaxing, his cell phone rang, and he answered. William recognised the voice: it was Sherene.

Sherene identified herself as *Tarmac* and asked him for money. He told her he did not have any money and that ended their conversation. She called him sometime later but this time she offered him sex. He told her that he was an old man and could not afford to pay her rates for sex but he would give her $10.00. About an hour later, Sherene came to William's shop and he gave her $10.00. While there, Sherene told him she used drugs, but never said what types of drugs she used.

After that time, William would receive several calls from Sherene, always asking for money. Occasionally William would call Sherene to let her know he had some money for her; occasionally, he would return her calls, but the requests were always the same: money. If he had, William would let her know when she could pass for the funds.

According to him, he never had sex with Sherene after the churchyard encounter and she only collected money from him. He said even though he later found out that she was, in Bajan parlance, a 'paro', he still gave her money because he pitied her. He described Sherene as a woman who dressed well and always behaved like a lady.

Rape ordeal

Another man from Sherene's past came up on the police 'radar'. The two had first crossed paths a few years earlier.

On April 16th, 2005, around 12:45 a.m., Sherene left home to go by a friend who lived in Dover. At the time she was living with her boyfriend Derek Louis. Just as she was about to go into her friend's house, a silver-grey car pulled up next to her on her left side and she heard a voice asking: *"Hey, wuh you doing now?"*

Sherene turned and looked in the car to see who was addressing her and recognised that it was a man she had met before, but his name eluded her at the time. She remembered meeting him in December 2004 at her friend's house and then seeing him again in March 2005.

"Nothing," she said.

"Come and get a smoke," he encouraged.

"Alright," she agreed and got into the car.

The man drove across the ABC Highway and headed to Wavell Avenue in Black Rock, St Michael. The man stopped and parked at the back of a man's house and the two got out and smoked for about ten to fifteen minutes. She admitted later to police that it was a 'rock' (crack cocaine) she was smoking. While they were smoking, the man asked her if she had ever had anal sex and if she sucks d*** (performs oral sex).

"No, I ain't pun all dat foolishness."

The man then told her he would pay her $80.00 to have anal sex with her.

"Cah me back wey you get me from. I does do my thing. I does mek my money on the street," she told him.

Sherene and the man walked back to the car, got in and drove off, but Sherene had made a mental note of the license plate number before she got in. The man drove to the 'T'-junction at Black Rock Main Road, and turned right, heading in a northerly direction and not left in the direction of Christ Church.

"Why are you going this way?" she queried.

I gine and visit a friend first," he said, and kept driving.

He continued along Black Rock Main Road, turned right and headed up St. Stephen's Hill before turning left towards the traffic lights at Hinds Hill. At that junction, the man kept straight, passing Queen's College and Haynesville and making his way down to Holders Hill. He continued making a lot of twists and turns through dark roads and eventually started to scare her. *"I hope you ain't carrying me too far away to Faraway Land,"* she said.

The man finally stopped and cut the engine. Sherene took in her surroundings and saw that he had parked the car on the right side of a hut, facing out. The hut had a light on the outside and it was switched on.

After seeing him turn off the engine, she asked, *"Why you come up here?"*

He quickly grabbed her by the front of her dress and pulled a cutlass from between the two front seats and swung it at her. *"Why you freaking out so?"* he shouted.

Sherene later told police that she began to scream at this point and had put up her left hand, grabbed his hand that held the cutlass and pleaded with him not to kill her. *"Don't kill me! Don't hurt me! It ain't got to come to this. I gine do whatever you want,"* she begged, trembling with fear.

He held her dress with his left hand and the cutlass with his right hand.

Fearing for her life, she started to tremble.

She told herself that he was armed with a cutlass, and she would do whatever he asked because she did not want him to kill her.

After a moment, he released her, got out of the car with the cutlass still in his hand, and walked around the car from the back. When he came to her side of the car, he ordered her to get out and to take off her panty. Sherene complied. She got out of the car, took off her panty and dropped it on the ground. The man picked it up and, grabbing her by the front of her dress, pulled her across the garden, under a tree. He then took off his pants and boxer shorts and, she related afterwards, started telling her all manner of sexually degrading things. *"Suck this c***, lick my b****, mek love to me like you mekking love to you man,"* he ordered.

He forced her to perform oral sex on him and then he did the same to her. After that, he had sex with her, at one point placing the top of the cutlass inside her vagina. After he took out the cutlass, the man raped her again.

After raping her, he got up and told her to wash off by a nearby pipe.

He then took her home. Sherene did not report the matter at the time.

On Monday, August 25th, 2005, sometime after 11:00 pm, Sherene was walking towards Paradise Village when she recognised the car parked outside her friend's house. It was the same silver-grey car of the man who had raped her in April.

After confirming the car had the same registration number she turned around and walked to Top Rock service station and used the phone. She called the police emergency number and explained to the policewoman on the line what she was calling about. She was transferred to the Worthing Police Station. A few minutes later, police arrived at Top Rock, and Sherene directed them to the silver-grey car, still parked in front of her friend's home. However, the man was not in the car. The police then spoke to Sherene's friend who told them that the driver was inside. When he eventually came out, Sherene immediately pointed him out to the police as the man who had raped her. The police asked him if he heard what she said and told him of his rights.

"What I do?" he asked and the police asked him to come with them to Worthing Police Station. The man's name was Winston Shoman and he was arrested and charged for the rape of Sherene Gooding.

At the time of Sherene's murder, Winston Shoman was on bail for raping Sherene

Police were looking hard at Shoman. Sherene's identification of him to police for the crime of raping her under threat of cutlass chops was definitely a motive Winston Shoman was considered a man of interest in this case.

Derek Matthews and Derek Louis

At one point, Sherene was involved with two men who had the same first name: Derek Matthews and Derek Louis.

Derek Matthews

Derek Matthews seemed to be the 'Derek' who presented the more relationship problems. He was identified as the one who inflicted injuries on Sherene. He scarred her repeatedly and threatened to kill her. Police investigations also revealed that he had a deep infatuation with her long after their relationship had ended.

Matthews, a career criminal, was described as a man with a mental history who had been prescribed medication for most of his adult life. He was also described as having a propensity to violence and had to be segregated from the prison population while he was incarcerated. One man who was interviewed by police said that during his conversations with Sherene, she would tell him about her life experiences. On one occasion, she told him of being attacked by Derek Matthews who stabbed her in the throat. She also told him that Derek had told her he intended to finish the job.

Derek Matthews was a man of interest to the police.

Derek Louis

The other '*Derek*' – Derek Louis – was a self-employed landscaper for approximately twenty years and the father of two children. About fifteen years before Sherene's death, Louis began to use cocaine. He frequented the Maxwell Hill area in Christ Church for his drugs .

Sometime in September, 2003, while in Maxwell, Christ Church sitting on a large rock next to a track, he met Sherene, whom he knew by her street name *Tarmac*. He had seen her previously on the block and later described her as the type of person that, when drunk, would start to curse and carry on, making a lot of noise.

On this particular night, she approached him and sat beside him, drinking alcohol, and hitting cocaine. Derek stated that they started to talk to each other, as he had approached her about buying sex as he knew she was a prostitute. He eventually invited her back to his house and she agreed. At his home, they had sex and he then brought her back to the block. She told him she wanted to see him again and they eventually reconnected and became intimately involved. When Louis met her, she was living with a man. After he and Sherene became involved, she spent most of her time at his residence in St Joseph but returned to her Maxwell abode periodically as most of her clothing was still there at the boyfriend's house. Sherene started to complain about her boyfriend and eventually moved in with Louis. Sometimes, she spent two to three days at his house. At other times she would leave one day and return the following morning.

Louis said he was in love with Sherene, and she with him. He said he would look out for her and make sure that she was okay, but he would not normally give her money as she would have her own, and he would have his. If he had money to spare, he would give her, but he would not do this often, as he could not afford her drug habit and his own. He stated that Sherene was a heavy user and would require a lot of drugs until she was satisfied that she had enough. She would come home, sleep it off and return for more. Louis noted that he and Sherene had an understanding as it related to her way of life, and he accepted that she was a drug user (like he was) and was also into prostitution.

On the face of it, Louis didn't look to be in the frame for Sherene's murder but police were not prepared to rule him out yet. Sure, he seemed to accept his girlfriend's way of life but it would be unusual for such a situation to sit well with a man who claimed to be in love.

+++++++++

Kristen, while not a prime suspect, was interviewed and gave some insight into the aggression displayed by Sherene.

Like Sherene, Kristen was a cocaine user and for a brief while before Sherene, had been involved sexually with Derek Louis. Kristen and Sherene did not have a friendly relationship. Kristen claimed that Sherene always threatened to beat her up if she talked to Louis. She claimed that Sherene was loud and aggressive, and always wanted to beat on her.

She and Sherene were also both sexually involved with a man named Jack, though not at the same time. She said that Sherene was jealous of her relationship with Jack because when she (Kristen) was with him, Sherene was not allowed to visit his house. She started sleeping at a man named Oscar's house where she would also shower. Kristen said she found that arrangement strange as she knew Sherene was involved with Derek Louis. She stated that Sherene was always ready to curse out Derek, while he, on the other hand, would not raise his voice but try to calm her down and take her home. She never saw Louis become aggressive towards Sherene.

Kristen told the police that because of Sherene's behaviour and threats of bodily harm, she avoided her. According to Kristen, Sherene's last outburst was in December of 2004 when she slapped her in her face for no reason.

Is fear for one's life a motive for murder? Yes, but as there were no recent flare-ups of threats or actual assault, Kristen was not considered a suspect for this crime

But the question is, were there any other women out there *like* Kristen who, having been threatened and/or beaten by Sherene, feared for their life enough to murder Sherene?

Police continued their investigations. Interviews were conducted, alibis were received and these were then duly checked.

The relationship between Louis and Sherene was questionable. Although Sherene lived at his home, the relationship, as outlined previously, was not the smoothest. Days would pass and Derek would not see hide nor hair of Sherene.

When asked about his movements in the days leading up to the discovery of Sherene's body, Derek provided police with the following details of his whereabouts.

April 5th

Derek Louis woke up about 6:50 a.m., along with Sherene. She cooked, they ate and then he left home for work around 1:30 p.m. Sherene was at home. He rode his bicycle to the home of one of his landscaping clients in Welches Terrace, St Michael. After work, he rode back home arriving around 7:00 p.m.

When he got home, Sherene was there with his sisters watching television. He spoke to her, touched her head, and told her he was home. She eventually joined him in his bedroom said she felt like smoking. He took his tools off the bicycle and he and Sherene showered and dressed. At the time, she was wearing a long black skirt, with two red stripes down the sides, and two small splits at each side, a black armhole blouse with a design covering the entire blouse.

He and Sherene left home together on his bicycle and rode to Maxwell, Christ Church getting there around 7:30 p.m. They got some drugs to smoke and stood in the roadway. Sherene left him and went to the residence of a man he only knew as 'Oscar' to use the bathroom and returned shortly after. Sherene then started to play a card game with a guy called Cat. He (Louis) was in the road while she played cards. Ten minutes later, he told her he was ready to go home as all the money he had was gone. He had $40.00 and gave her $20.00. She told him she would walk him through *the line* that was a track between two houses and led back to the main road. They walked through the line and when they reached the main road she told him that she would come home when she was ready, or she would call and he could come and meet her. Sherene told him she was going back by Oscar to get something to smoke and he climbed on his bicycle and rode away. This was the last time he saw Sherene alive.

He went home and called his friend Karl and told him that he was coming over to his house. He hung up, got on his bicycle, and rode to Karl's residence. When he arrived there, they left in a car which he was fixing as Karl was a mechanic, and they drove to a minimart where he purchased food items and beers.

They then returned to his residence, where they drank beers and 'had a good time'. He slept at Karl's residence.

April 6th

He left Karl's house at 6:00 a.m. and returned home. He spent the day in bed sleeping and woke at about 2:00 p.m. He did not see Sherene and did not ask anyone in the house for her. This was normal behaviour for her and he knew that once he did not see her out there, she had not returned home yet. He took a shower, got something to eat and returned to bed. He did not leave home for the rest of that day and Sherene did not return.

April 7th

Derek woke up, took a shower, and got something to eat. He then left home on his bicycle and went to Graeme Hall, Christ Church to cut a lawn for a client. He finished about 3:30 p.m., packed up his tools and rode home, making one stop to purchase a kite for his son from a vendor along the roadway. Arriving home, he took a shower, got dressed and left at about 8:00 p.m. He rode to where his son lived, delivered the kite and spent about an hour with him.

After leaving his son, he went to 'The Big House', the name of the place where they bought drugs. He remained at The Big House until 4:30 a.m. and then rode home. No one was awake when he arrived home and he went to bed.

April 8-12

Over the next few days, Derek went about his life in his usual fashion, working when there was work, smoking when he had money and staying home when he had none. Sometimes he would lime by the Big House and sometimes at Karl's home.

He told police that during this time he began to worry a bit about Sherene but not to the extent that he tried to call her or ascertain her whereabouts. He knew that she had been making plans to head to the country to visit her best friend so he figured she had gone without him.

April 13th

Derek slept at Karl the previous night, the 12th, and remained there the next day. Around 8:00 that night, he and Karl went to Maxwell Hill where Karl asked one of the men if he had seen Sherene. The man responded, *"Not for a little while."*

They then left Maxwell and drove back to Karl's house and while there, he asked Karl if Sherene had just disappeared off the face of the earth. He had become a lot more worried because he knew Sherene would normally visit the block as she was a very heavy drug user.

Despite his worry, he did not attempt to contact her or to find her as he felt she was playing a game by not calling. He decided that two could play that game and he did not call.

He again spent the night at Karl's residence.

April 14th and 15th

Derek and Karl spent the next two days together. They worked on cars at Karl's home and also in St. Philip. At one point, Derek gave Karl $20.00 so that he could purchase two cocaine rocks in Maxwell. When Karl returned he said he had not seen Sherene. Derek still had not tried to reach her by phone. He spent the night of the 15th at Karl's home.

April 16ᵗʰ

After waking up about 9:30 a.m., Derek said he took a bath, drank some hot tea and got something to smoke as he and Karl had decided they were not working that day. They cooked, ate and relaxed for the remainder of the day.

Later that evening, Karl left and returned a few hours later, running through the house shouting: *"They find the red pole dead!"*

Even though Derek knew that by "red pole" Karl meant Sherene, he still asked, *"Who you mean? Do you mean Sherene?"*

"Yes," Karl said.

Derek asked him if it was true, and he said he heard it from a friend of theirs and police were in the area asking questions about her.

The seven o'clock evening news started, and Karl turned up the television and he and Derek heard the news. (Derek later told the police that he was in shock and could not speak.) He then told himself that it could be true, as he had not seen or heard Sherene for a while, longer than normal for her.

He sat in silence for a while and eventually went to bed.

As police investigations continued apace, suspects were questioned; friends, acquaintances, *clients*, anyone with ties to Sherene and stories followed up. As the information came in, investigators whittled down their suspect pool to two high-level suspects: Derek Matthews and Winston Shoman.

Unfortunately, however, the information gathered could not connect the victim to either of these men *recently*.

Given the information that came in and their observations, investigators requested a psychiatric report on Derek Matthews, the 37-year-old ex-boyfriend from St Joseph.

Matthews had a history of a previous admission to the Psychiatric Hospital. He had been brought there because he threatened a neighbour who had hit one of his animals with a big rock. Police investigations also revealed that he had cut off the head of a dog in the neighbourhood. When asked directly if he had killed Sherene, Matthews said that the people in his district would say, *"Not he!"* meaning himself. He also stated that his neighbours would say that he is home all the time.

Matthews readily talked about Sherene and recounted to police his relationship with her. His account related that he met her in the Ivy while he was living in St Barnabas. About three months into the relationship, he asked her to move in with him. She agreed and they lived together for about one year between 2002 and 2003. Matthews said that during their relationship, Sherene asked him to tattoo her nickname on her chest. He was accustomed to inking tattoos on his own body so it was not an outlandish request and he tattooed the word *'Tarmac'* on her chest. He admitted that the relationship would become physically abusive "on occasions." He became aware that Sherene used cocaine when she told him two months into the relationship. According to him, this did not deter him from continuing their relationship. He said he loved her very much and that he believed he could help her stop her cocaine addiction. Most of their arguments arose from the fact that he wanted Sherene to stay at home in St Joseph to cook and clean instead of going to Paradise Village to buy cocaine.

He said that throughout their relationship, Sherene would continually visit Paradise Village to buy cocaine. He tried to encourage her to get a job, but she told him, *"My pussy does work for me."* He claimed that this made him very angry, but he did not hit her. He described Sherene as a very outspoken person who would tell him anything no matter how it hurt him. He stated that he could not stop Sherene from selling herself, but he kept insisting that he did not want to share her. He told the police that he would give her between $200.00 and $300.00 a week hoping that this would stop her from being a prostitute. Sherene, however, always wanted more money and he believed that this was to support her cocaine habit.

About four months into their relationship, Sherene became involved with a man named Andy, a Barbadian man who was married to a white English millionaire. Sherene told Matthews of her relationship with Andy but explained that she loved him (Matthews) and was only using Andy for his money. She told him that Andy would give her much more money than he could. However, Andy died months later in 2003. On the day of Andy's death, Sherene came to Matthews' job site and told him that she woke up and found Andy dead and that he had hung himself. When he saw Sherene, her face was swollen as if she was beaten. He asked her what happened to her face, and she told him that Andy had beaten her because she wanted to leave his home and he did not want her to go.

Matthews stated that the relationship with Sherene ended sometime in February or March 2003. Following their breakup, he visited Sherene about five to six times in 2003. By then she was living with a rastaman which the police later realised was Derek Louis. One weekend in 2003,

Derek told the police that he went to Paradise Village looking for Sherene. She was there and they talked for a while about their relationship. When it started to get dark outside, Sherene told him that she was going up the road and that he should go home. He told Sherene that he was not leaving until she returned. After some time, he did not see Sherene return.

About 1:00 a.m., he saw a man he knew as Laugher, who was a cocaine addict and smoked with Sherene in Paradise Village. He asked Laugher if he knew where Sherene was and he told him that he would show him. He paid Laugher $10.00 for the information. Laugher and Matthews walked to a wooden house on a hill. He told Laugher to shout for Sherene because if he did, she would not answer. Laugher shouted for Sherene's name, and she came out. Sherene was surprised to see Matthews and asked him what he was doing there. He told her that he was in Paradise Village waiting for her and she was in a house with a man. He told her to come with him and she told him to go home. A rastaman came out and joined Sherene, asking Matthews if he did not hear what Sherene said. According to him, the situation made him very angry, and he walked away. He did not know the rastaman's name or who he was as he had never seen him before.

According to Matthews, when he reached the gas station at Top Rock, he saw a bottle and he broke it. He planned on stabbing Sherene with the bottle when he saw her again.

Morning came and he eventually saw Sherene in Paradise Village, but by that time his anger had subsided. He told Sherene to come and go home but she still refused. He stayed in Paradise Village all day until night came, when he saw Sherene about to get into a car. Sherene saw him also and said, *"Why you don't go home, you black bitch!"* He said this made him so angry that he went for the same bottle which he had thrown on the ground earlier and he stabbed her in the face. Sherene was taken to the hospital by ambulance, and he was later charged by the police. However, Sherene dropped the case against him. According to him, *"Sherene loved me. Sherene and I started our relationship over."*

Within a few weeks, however, Sherene started to prostitute herself again. Matthews said he tried to make the relationship work, but Sherene did not want it. He continued trying to convince her. He would visit the house she was staying with the rastaman asking her to come home. He told the police that nine months had passed since he had seen or heard Sherene as he had stopped going to Paradise Village. Over the years, however, he would visit the village where she was staying with the rastaman a few times and saw Sherene three or four times sitting in the area he referred to as a 'dope hole'. According to Matthews, the men all looked like paros.

On one of the occasions he visited there, Sherene told him that she had been raped by a rastafarian who had picked her up from the same area and took her to St James. She told him the man raped her and tried to cut off her head with a cutlass, but she was able to beg for her life. He did not remember the date or time she told him this. Matthews said that on April 19th, 2007, he was outside painting his house when his mother came and told him that she understood that the body found days earlier was Sherene's. He stood in shock and could not continue with the painting job.

On Saturday, April 21st, 2007, he decided that he wanted to see the body for himself to be convinced that Sherene was dead. Around 11:00 a.m. he took it upon himself to go to the Queen Elizabeth Hospital morgue where he was met by an orderly. He told the orderly that he wanted to see the body that had been found with its head off. He did not explain *why* he wanted to see it. The orderly told him that the body was not there and that Two Sons Funeral Home had it. He decided not to go to the funeral home. He left the morgue and went to Nelson Street and according to him, *"picked a fare,"* the Barbadian vernacular for having sex with a sex worker. He felt that the police were trying to pin Sherene's murder on him because they could not find the man who, to use his words, *"breed she."*

Matthews, who claimed he was in a relationship at the time that Sherene was murdered, said that he had an alibi for the estimated timeframe of the death.

At this point, Matthews was made aware that a psychiatrist had been asked to review and analyze a copy of a book given to her by the police, the original of which was in their possession.

Matthews said that he had placed Sherene's name in his book as it was his habit to write down the names of *"people that get kill"* in that book. He also wrote down his sleeping dreams in that book. He added that on the date of the psychiatric interview, he made no entries into the book because it was in the possession of the police. Dreams, he indicated, would be entered into the book as soon as he awoke so that he would not forget them. The book was almost full of 'X's. Matthews recounted that each X was a dream and that dreams were both bad and good. He could not pinpoint any particular X in the book and state what dream it represented. He was also asked about a particular phrase that was written on one of the pages of the book: *"No let de people know dat they"* but he could not say what that was about or why he wrote it.

He referred to this book as his 'True Life Book' and stated that the contents mainly *"come from the news and are printed in the paper."* He advised that things in the book were not written in any order. He wrote on any page and every page. He again referred to his deceased ex-girlfriend saying that she was killed on a Wednesday, but he put down the 18th. That Wednesday was the 16th. Matthews noted that the person who killed Sherene deserved to die. He also spoke of another murder that had taken place saying that the person who killed Sherene was also the same person who killed a schoolgirl. It is not on record to which schoolgirl or murder he was referring. He went on to say that keys and a knife were found next to the schoolgirl and there was blood next to her body. Matthews also told police that an ID card was found next to Sherene. He stated that all of that meant that the same person did both murders, which the psychiatrist believed was an illogical thought process.

Matthews was asked about drug use. He admitted to smoking cigarettes but emphatically denied using marijuana or cocaine, and said that he hardly ever used alcohol. He admitted to having relationships since Sherene, but not steady like his relationship with Sherene. The psychiatrist said that Matthews stuck close to his story but at many points during the interview, he was illogical in his thought processes. He denied killing any big animal and said that he would not kill anything which needed to live like him. He described himself as a rasta from the heart.

From his mental examination, Matthews was deemed as coherent though somewhat illogical at times and seemed to protest a bit much about things that had not even been discussed at the time. He was deemed as being preoccupied with killing and death.

The contents of Matthews' book were studied by three mental health officers: two psychiatrists and a psychologist. Psychiatrist number one viewed the book's organisation as psychotic. The preoccupation with killing was also noted. Psychiatrist number two described the book's content as bizarre and the organisation as obsessional in nature. While the main theme was death and killing, love and separation issues were others identified. Matthews had also written down many phallic symbols.

The psychologist identified obsession, aggression and attention to detail (brought out by the way the symbols were embedded) as likely personality traits of the book's owner. The love theme and phallic nature of some symbols were similarly noted. The psychologist noted that there were some parental issues identified and sexuality issues seemed apparent. There was some degree of preservation towards the end of the book. Collectively and independently, these therapists felt that Matthews was a dangerous individual who was prone to using illegal substances. These substances would cause him to become more aggressive. These therapists considered Matthews as someone who should be monitored as he could constitute a danger to others and a danger to himself.

Had police found their killer?

Police picked up Winston Shoman, the man who was charged for the rape of Sherene, for questioning and the following information was gleaned. Winston Shoman was deported to Barbados in 1993 after serving a custodial sentence in the United Kingdom for rape, theft, burglary, and robbery. Shoman lived with his wife at the time of his arrest for Sherene's rape.

He was a cocaine user and admitted that he had gone to a dealer named Thelston to buy cocaine in 2005 and met up on Sherene there. He bought $100.00 in cocaine rocks and started smoking. He offered Sherene a smoke and they started talking. He asked her if she "does play," referring to prostituting herself, and she responded in the affirmative. He told her that he had $40.00, and she said, *Okay, but not here,* referring to Thelston's residence. His version of events was similar to Sherene's with regards to going to her house in Maxwell, Christ Church. He said he gave her the money and they smoked. He said he was too high and could not get an erection, so he told her he was going home. He said he then left. About a week after that, he went again to Thelston's place, but he had no money and Thelston would not trust him with the cocaine. When he was leaving, he saw Sherene again, who asked him if he had anything to smoke and he said no. He then told her he was going by a friend who lived in Black Rock to get something to smoke, and asked her if she wanted to come. She got into the car and the two set out.

He then told police that he drove to his friend's residence in Black Rock and got six cocaine rocks from him. They left there and went to Sandy Lane and on into Dukes, St Thomas. He said they arrived there somewhere between 2:00 a.m. and 3:00 a.m., smoked and had sex. He told police that he fell asleep afterwards and when he woke up, it was morning. The car did not have much gas and he could not take her back to Christ Church.

He said he dropped her off at the bottom of Highway 2A for her to go by her family and he then went home.

Shoman recalled that a few months later, sometime in August 2005, he was by Thelston when the police came there. As he came outside, he saw Sherene and she said, *"It is him!"* He was arrested and subsequently charged with rape. He said that because of this, his wife moved out and the rent and the bills were too much for him, so he was also forced to move out. Shoman stated that he went back to Thelston shortly after and told him that he had not raped Sherene. He also asked Thelston to talk to her to see if she would discontinue the case. Shortly after that, someone else who frequented Thelston's residence told him that Sherene said that she has a man in court, and she will get $25,000.00 off him.

In early 2006, while he was at Thelston, he saw Sherene. According to Shoman, Sherene told him, *"You ain't digging nothing, right?"* He looked at her and did not say anything to her and according to him, he just walked away. Shoman said he had not seen Sherene since then. On April 19th, 2007, he was at a residence in Vauxhall, Christ Church when his aunt called him. She informed him that the lady who had him in court for rape was found dead. He went and bought a paper to see for himself. He then called his wife and told her about the article in the paper. He told the police he had nothing to do with Sherene's death and at no time did he make any threats against her. He told the police he was working at the residence daily from 7:00 a.m. to 6:00 p.m. When he finished work, he would go to his friend's place and then go home.

His friend confirmed this.

In summary, through their investigations, police tried to piece together a picture of Sherene's lifestyle and movement just prior to her murder.

Sherene was addicted to crack cocaine and maintaining her drug habit was more important than commitment to relationships. With mainstream employment no longer an option, Sherene turned to prostitution and soon realised that prostitution paid the bills.

She plied her 'trade' – her body – through Dover, Christ Church and later Maxwell in the same parish. Clients would pick her up on the main road, refraining from making contact in the various drug areas she frequented. Her cell phone was her communication hub. Her behaviour was seemingly accepted by her lovers in the unique relationships she cultivated.

Though Sherene walked the road like a 'paro', she did not carry herself in the stereotypical way – unwashed and unkempt. On the contrary, her clean exterior belied the dark world of illegal drugs and prostitution in which she engaged.

There was evidence that there was no set routine for Sherene but rather her movements were largely controlled by her vice for cocaine rocks and alcohol. When satisfied, she would visit her Gall Hill home with her boyfriend Derek Louis, especially on Sundays. But Sherene saw the people in the drug holes as her family. Evidence showed that there was no closeness to her family locally or in North America, though the members overseas would communicate with her via landline from a resident in the Maxwell area.

Sherene was an outpatient at the Randall Matthews and St John poly-clinics, and this was as a result of her first pregnancy. There was no information on any private care treatment. There was an incident of psychiatric care due to an application made by the Magistrate's Court for a shoplifting offence. The report from the Psychiatric Hospital indicated that she had no desire to accept drug rehabilitation and there were no other avenues to assist her. It also should be noted that she left one child at the QEH after birth and another child with a family member after saying to that family member that she would return in an hour.

Over one hundred people were interviewed in connection with Sherene Gooding's murder and each of them had a different relationship with Sherene. Yet strangely, with all the possible motives and potential leads in the case, no one has been identified as Sherene's killer.

While police deemed that the motive for the murder was inconclusive, many possibilities have been highlighted in this chapter.

In the end, the mix of drug addiction, prostitution, jealousy, fear and violence proved to be lethal.

Her head was never recovered.

CHAPTER NINE

Who Would Have Killed Poor Isalene?

T he horror of sexual violence always seems to hit harder when perpetrated against the elderly. This is not to mitigate in any way the same
acts inflicted on younger people but our minds reel as we instinctively
assume – often correctly – that the fragility of older folk makes them even
more vulnerable to these heinous attacks.

There is a pervasive stereotype that younger women are usually the
victims of rape or sexual assault. However, research has shown that there
are many people, far too many over 60 years old, who are also victims of
sexual violence.

Imagine, having worked hard over the years, these esteemed persons
of our soil have made their contributions, and looking forward to their
retirement to enjoy their sunset years.

Only to be brutally targeted.

Eighty-two year old pensioner Mrs. Isalene Harris lived in a wall-con-
structed house with a shop attached near to St Leonard's Avenue in St
Michael. She was alone in her home as her husband Alistair Harris had
died in 2008 and her son Ryan lived overseas.

Isalene suffered from hypertension and spinal arthritis, but apart from
these ailments, she was in reasonable health for her age, was ambulant
and still able to physically look after herself. Despite that, family friends
would still visit occasionally to look in on her and ensure that all was well.
They would assist Isalene with chores, operating the shop, cashing her
pension cheques and paying her bills.

Mrs. Harris was well known in the area and her shop, known as 'Harris
Bar', was a landmark in the district and the preferred location for dances
and other functions. A sociable person, Mrs. Harris was loved and
respected by the people who knew her.

Since her husband passed just under two years earlier, Isalene spent
most of her time at home where she still operated the shop but on a much
smaller scale than in its heyday. She only sold a few items including soft
drinks, beers, small bottles of rum and loose cigarettes from a container.
She would serve a few customers from the verandah at the front of the

residence instead of opening the shop doors. The business did not make any large sums of money and what profit there was, was small.

On Sundays, Mrs. Harris would prepare lunch for some of her friends who attended the St Leonard's Church, and she would open the shop to entertain these persons. She spent a lot of her time in the verandah, retiring to bed at varying times of the night depending on whether or not she had company. Occasionally, a family friend might sleep over but she mostly slept in the house alone.

She was last seen alive at her residence by her neighbour Robert, about 11:15 p.m. on January 2nd, 2010.

In the mid to latter part of 2009, there were unusually high incidences of criminal activity in the community and the police were kept especially busy due to the numerous cases of burglaries being reported. The high point – or low point – of the criminal activity in the area was the murder of 95-year-old William Phillips of St Leonards' Avenue, Westbury Road, St Michael. His residence was ransacked, and an undetermined amount of money stolen. Mr. Phillips' lifeless body was found in his bedroom bound to his bed. The police hypothesized that burglary was the likely motive for the crime. Since then, three men were arrested and charged for his murder.

Isalene's body discovered

On January 3rd, 2010, persons who went to visit Mrs. Harris observed that the left section of the sliding door of her home was opened. There was no response from Mrs. Harris to calls made by them. Concerned, Sophia, a longtime friend of Isalene, who was also one of her neighbours, decided to call the Red Cross in case Mrs. Harris needed some sort of medical assistance.

When the medics arrived about 12:10 p.m, Sophia entered the house accompanied by Mr. Aldo Babb, a medic who worked with the Red Cross.

As she entered the house Sophia did not see Isalene so she headed for the bedroom to find her friend.

There, she made the grim find.

Sophia found Isalene motionless on her bed with her head, face, hands and feet bound and abrasions on the left side of her face.

Sophia called to Mr. Babb who rushed to the bedroom. He checked for a pulse but there was none. As they exited the bedroom to call for the police and an ambulance, there were obvious signs that sections of the house was searched.

Once the police and ambulance were called, Sophia and Mr. Babb went outside and told the gathering crowd what had happened.

Ambulance attendants soon arrived on the scene. They checked the body and found no sign of life.

Isalene's body was lying on its back across the bed, her head facing the public road. Several curtains were also on the bed. The body was clad in a multi-coloured flowered duster that was open to the front. A panty was hanging on Isalene's right foot. The stitching in the waist of the panty appeared to have been torn as if this garment had been forcibly removed.

It appeared as if Mrs. Harris was sexually assaulted.

A gold-coloured curtain was tied around her head and face. The same curtain was used to tie her left hand onto her head. Her feet were tied with a yellow towel above the area where the panty hung. There was bruising on the left side of her face.

The murder scene

All three bedrooms in Isalene's home appeared to have been searched and a torn cream-coloured latex glove was found on the floor in the middle bedroom amongst some curtains. An unlit match was on the floor of the living room near the rug and the electricity was turned off at the circuit breaker in the dining area. A shoe print on the handle of a chair at the dining table made it appear as if someone had stood on the chair to reach the circuit breaker. A plastic container with a black cover containing loose cigarettes was on a chair in the living area and a Barbados $2.00 note lay beside the container.

At the scene, police carried out a thorough investigation but there were no signs of forced entry into the house or Mrs. Harris's bedroom. The police surmised that the culprit or culprits entered the house via the unsecured right half of the glass sliding door and disturbed Mrs. Harris while she was sleeping in her bedroom. She woke up to investigate and the culprit or culprits attacked her in the living or dining area, forced her to the bedroom and sexually assaulted her, or attempted to do so. The culprit or culprits tied her up, strangled her at some point, turned off the electricity and used the lamp to search the house. Some property was taken and he/they left the same way he/they had entered.

There seemed to be an attempt to set fire to the bedroom where the body was found. A lit kerosene oil lamp and what appeared to be pieces of burnt paper were found on the bedroom floor. There was also a strong smell of kerosene oil in the area. Fingerprints were found on the lamp and also on the glass sliding door. However, several curious people had visited the residence before the police had arrived. To this date, the prints found at the scene have not been identified. This led the police to believe that the prints might have been deposited by someone other than the culprits. What was clear was that the crime scene was compromised due to the human traffic that was moving through it.

Efforts were made to identify all persons who visited the residence and elimination prints were taken. Also, the prints of persons who were brought into custody were checked against those prints that were found. It is still unclear if all persons who visited the house out of curiosity were identified.

Exactly what property, if any, was stolen remains a mystery since Isalene was wearing her gold jewellery when the body was discovered.

A post-mortem carried out on the body of Isalene Harris on January 6th, 2010, by Dr David Gaskin, attributed cause of death to asphyxia (smothering). Dr. Gaskin also determined there was vaginal penetration. Vaginal swabs and nail clippings were taken and handed over to Sergeant Lindo who attended the post-mortem. The Government's Analyst Office conducted tests to ascertain if there was any forensic activity, such as DNA but the results were negative.

Because the forensic aspect of the investigation did not produce concrete evidence of sexual assault at the time of the attack, they could not narrow the investigations to potentially identified persons who were known gerontophiles.

Efforts were made to concentrate on burglars known to operate in districts near the crime scene and on the actual cases of burglary which were committed in these areas. The investigative plan was to find a link between those cases of burglary and murder, but no correlations were found.

Motive

The motive for Mrs. Harris's murder appeared initially to be burglary and as investigations continued, it became apparent that someone was in the habit of entering the residence and stealing small sums of money.

The police hypothesized that on this occasion, the culprit was disturbed by Mrs. Harris leading to her being physically assaulted and murdered.

Police conducted extensive house-to-house enquiries in the area bounded by Westbury Road, Pickwick Gap Main Road, 3rd Avenue Pickwick Gap and Harbour Road. No useful information was received from the persons interviewed.

Denise, a close family friend who visited the house about twice weekly to assist with running the shop, told police that Ryan, Isalene's son, had asked her to look after his mother since he was living overseas. She last visited Mrs. Harris on Tuesday, December 22nd, 2009, spending the night there and leaving the following day. Denise told the police that she had never seen Mrs. Harris using the right half of the sliding door and was not aware if that section of the door could be properly secured. She told investigators that she would sometimes sleep over at Mrs. Harris in her bedroom. She stated that Mrs. Harris would always sleep with her bedroom door bolted as a security measure. She would not use a lamp and the electricity to the house would normally be kept on.

Denise pointed out that the lamp found on the bedroom floor was kept on the dresser in the second bedroom. Mrs. Harris kept a beige plastic container with dollar coins and twenty-five cent pieces, and a cut 'Bico' ice cream container with ten cents, five cents and one cent pieces on the table in the dining area. These were for making change for customers.

Mrs. Harris had told her that one night in the early part of December 2009, someone stole $40.00 made up of one-dollar and twenty-five cent coins from the beige plastic container which was on the dining room table while she slept. She had found the container in the kitchen the following morning. There were no signs of forced entry to the house and Mrs. Harris never reported the matter to the police.

To assist officers, Denise searched the house and the shop to see if she might find any missing property. She discovered that Mrs. Harris' purse in which she kept paper money was missing from the house. This purse was described as green in colour, made of cloth type material with a curved top and a single zipper. It is not known how much money this purse contained but the information received was that Mrs. Harris had about Bds $300.00 remaining after paying for her husband's funeral. This money was never found. Also missing were two gold bangles with round heads. Denise told police that she was not familiar with all the items at the house including

Mrs. Harris's jewellery and other valuable property, or all items of stock in the shop, so the possibility existed that other items could be missing.

Sixty persons in total were interviewed, including an elderly man by the name of Rawle.

Rawle was a carpenter who did odd jobs for Mrs. Harris including the last job which was cleaning the windows and hanging Christmas lights for her in December 2009. He informed police that about two weeks before the murder, he was walking along the gap between 2:00 a.m and 2:30 a.m when he saw a young man riding a bicycle quickly along the same gap. When he got to Mrs. Harris' house, he saw that the right half of the sliding door was opened. He alerted Mrs. Harris and she checked and realised that while the electricity to her house was off, lights in the other houses were on. John, who lived in the area subsequently checked for Mrs. Harris only to realise that the electricity had been turned off *at the breaker*. Later that day he checked the sliding door and noticed that the lock to the right half of this door was not working. He placed a piece of wood into the track of the door to prevent it from opening. He also stated that Mrs. Harris had told him that she had missed some money from the dining room table sometime in December 2009. She told John that she had seen a shadow inside the house, and when she checked, she saw a slim, tall, "fair-skinned" young man run out of the shop, get onto a bicycle and ride away.

Robert Rollins and Roger Glenton were regular patrons of Mrs. Harris' shop. They would often sit outside at the front of the house during the evening and at night they talked with Mrs. Harris while drinking. On Saturday, January 2nd, 2010, they went to Mrs. Harris' shop as usual. This time they sat on the back of Robert's motor van and drank rum and coke while chatting with each other. Mrs. Harris was in the verandah. They both left about 11 p.m. to go home and as Mrs. Harris was still in the verandah, they called to her to say that they were leaving.

Robert Rollins stated that when he arrived at his house which was a short distance away, he looked from his verandah and saw Mrs. Harris in her verandah, alone, at about 11:15 p.m., which was unusual. He did not think much more of it, however, and continued to drink rum until he fell asleep. He found out about the murder the following day.

Investigations centred around persons known to be involved in burglaries in the general Westbury Road, President Kennedy Drive, Barbarees Hill, Eagle Hall, New Orleans and Baxter's Road areas. They were also mindful of the apparent sexual molestation of the victim, and so persons with a penchant for this type of act were also considered.

One person the police had their spotlight on was a tall young man named Ricky who was slimly built with a fair complexion and rode a bicycle. A man fitting this general description had been seen on a number of occasions, entering Mrs. Harris' unsecured residence at night and was stealing small sums of money.

Another young man, 39-year-old Anderson Morland of Westbury Road, St Michael was interviewed because information received from an unknown source indicated that he was responsible for the murder. Police determined that he was the main suspect in this matter. He came into police custody voluntarily on January 7th, 2010 and was interrogated. He provided police with a statement in connection with his movements between the morning of Saturday, January 2nd, 2010, and the morning of Sunday, January 3rd, 2010. He was a cocaine addict and he stated that he was using a bicycle and travelling between different areas of Bank Hall and New Orleans where he bought cocaine and used it in areas frequented by other addicts.

He also stated that he visited the residence of a man called Peter from a neighbouring community and participated in a homosexual acts during the night. His alibi was checked, and his prints were checked against those found at the scene but there was no match. While being interrogated, he admitted to being responsible for the murder. However, as he was being questioned regarding the circumstances, he was unable to speak with any intimacy of the details of the incident or anything at the scene. Police discovered that he had sold jewellery to a man in Bank Hall, St Michael who sold cocaine. Some items of jewellery were recovered from the man in Bank Hall, but none of them fit the description of anything stolen from Mrs. Harris.

Anderson Morland was subsequently released.

Other men in their 30s from Westbury Road, New Orleans, Pickwick Gap and even Husbands in St James, were also questioned as their names were mentioned as being responsible for the murder. They were interviewed, gave statements that were checked, and they were released.

Mrs. Harris had no close relatives in Barbados and only a few middle-aged friends who frequented her home. The information provided by them was not of an intimate enough nature to formulate an objective report. From police investigations, they believed that the victim's lifestyle or circumstances did not contribute to her demise.

Eleven years on and Isalene Harris' murder remains unsolved and unavenged. A well loved woman, who did not deserve to die like this, who just wanted to survive by modest means and help her friends are the accolades used to describe her.

With little hope for fresh evidence, it is hard to see how justice could be done for Isalene. For her family and friends, they are left to experience the intense and painful emotions of anger, frustration and sorrow knowing that their loved one's life was taken away in such a vicious, abhorrent and odious manner.

CHAPTER TEN

Forensic Dilemma: Who or What Killed Julia?

O n June 18th, 2011, the partially decomposed body of Julia Griffith, 20 years old, was discovered on a plot of land used for agricultural purposes in Christ Church, near the Grantley Adams International Airport. The area is popular among persons who watch aircraft landing, however, it doubled as a lovers' lane at night. There were no residences within the immediate vicinity and the area was usually desolate and had poor lighting.

The body was clad in a short dark coloured top with the logo Aeropostale to the front, black tights and beige underwear. The deceased was wearing a burgundy wig.

Who would have wanted Julia dead, and what was the motive?

Background

Julia was considered to be a sociable person who frequented many nightclubs in and out of the city. While attending these clubs, she would meet men, exchange contact information and form friendships. She became sexually involved with some of them. Some of these men would transport her to and from the club. Her main means of communication was a Blackberry Pearl cellular phone.

Investigations showed that Julia was in the habit of leaving home, sometimes for days and not saying anything to her mother with whom she lived. When chided, she would respond by saying that she was an adult and that persons should not be concerned about what she did with her life. There were two sides to Julia's personality. People outside of her community knew her to be aggressive and one who was never afraid to become involved in verbal exchange. In stark contrast, those in her neighbourhood found her to be a soft-spoken person, who they never heard even raise her voice and were shocked at the horrific way in which she died.

On June 13th 2011, Julia left her mother Brenda's house without saying where she was going. When she did not return that night, her mother did not think anything of it and therefore did not report her missing. The following day, on June 14th, Julia's neighbour found a set of keys along the track which led to Julia's home and which he recognised to be Julia's. He handed them to another neighbour, who handed them to her mother. Brenda then tried calling Julia but did not get through to her. On June 16th, 2011 Brenda reported to the police that Julia was missing. On June 18th, some farmers working on a plot of land at Wilcox, Christ Church discovered a decomposed body which was later identified as that of Julia.

A postmortem examination was performed on the body by pathologist Dr David Gaskin on June 23rd, 2011 but the cause of death was not ascertained due to the state of decomposition.

Airport runway near to where the body of Julia was found

Police Investigations

Police believed that Julia was attacked in the area where her items were found, or the items were purposely placed there in an effort to mislead the investigation. The area was pointed out to police from the Northern Division and the area was searched but nothing was found. There was no evidence to suggest that a scuffle took place there.

A former workmate of Julia's told the police that she saw Julia on Wednesday, June 15th or Thursday, June 16th after 7:00 p.m. at Montrose, Christ Church. Julia was reportedly sitting in the passenger seat of a dark car which was beside the road. An unknown man was sitting in the front car. She was speaking to a Lisa from Montrose at the time. Lisa was interviewed but she denied seeing and speaking to Julia on that day.

The police also received information that a yellow van similar to a Parsons pest control van along with a white car was seen travelling along Wilcox Road on the night of June 17, 2011, and the drivers were acting suspiciously. The car turned off the main road, and onto the dirt road along where the body was found. The driver of the van missed the dirt road and the van almost flipped. This information was checked by police investigators without success.

Airport runway near to where the body of Julia was found

Exhumation of body

In their quest to ascertain the cause of death, investigators had the body exhumed on July 12th, 2011 from Mount Pleasant burial grounds where her body was interred. In accordance with policy, the Ministry of Health was represented by a health officer, representatives from Sanitation Service Authority, a tractor operator from a construction company unearthed the grave and representatives from a mortuary service removed the body and took it to the morgue of the Queen Elizabeth Hospital and returned it to

Mount Pleasant memorial. The body was escorted by police personnel on both occasions.

A forensic pathologist from Trinidad and Tobago, Dr Hughvon Des Vignes travelled to Barbados and performed a second examination of the body that same day but still could not determine the cause of death due to the degree of decomposition and the application of various materials to the body before burial. Dr Des Vignes was of the opinion, however, that Julia did not die of natural causes. There was an examination and dissection of the neck and windpipe which did not reveal any evidence consisting of manual strangulation. He opined that there was still the possibility that she could have died from smothering, defined as hands over nose and mouth, strangulation with a soft ligature or throttling (application of a chokehold) or arm lock against the windpipe.

A portion of Julia's liver was obtained for toxicology examination and a portion of muscle tissue was obtained for DNA analysis. They were handed over to Constable Grace and submitted to Dr Des Vignes and taken to Trinidad and Tobago by Constable Grace from the Forensic Scenes of Crime Unit for testing. However, to date the results of those tests are unknown.

Julia's partners

Several men with whom Julia was suspected to have been involved with were sought and interviewed by investigators, but none of them admitted to knowing how Julia met her death. Some of the persons interviewed included a number of men who were intimately involved with Julia at the time of her death.

Marston John

One young man, Marston, an airport employee was interviewed at Oistins Police Station on June 18th, 2011. He said that he met Julia a year and a half earlier on the social communication and dating site *Tagged*. They started communicating via this network and exchanged contact information. They started dating and this led to a sexual relationship. He considered her to be his girlfriend and they would spend time at each other's residence. However, to his dislike, she was in the habit of frequenting nightclubs and parties and on many occasions, she would not inform him of her whereabouts. He observed that she received calls and messages on her cell phone, and these messages appeared to be from men who supposedly wished to see Julia. He would sometimes take away the phone and check it, which led to arguments between them.

During the month of January 2011, she told him she was pregnant with twins after a doctors visit. He was elated. Sometime later, Julia developed pain in one of her sides and she visited a doctor on the advice of her mother. She told him that the doctor gave her five pills to take one time. Later, he and Julia went to get an ultrasound and during that ultrasound, they were both told that there was nothing in her belly. He believed that she aborted the pregnancy, which she denied.

The relationship went awry with them having disagreements over each other's mannerisms and financial issues. She would call him cheap because, according to him, one week she would ask for money to do her hair and the next week money for clothes. He recounted that he would often tell her that she could not get money like that all the time. The relationship ended in February 2011, but they occasionally spoke on the cellphone afterwards. He said he deleted her Blackberry BB pin from his phone, and she did the same. They however spoke on the cellphone occasionally after that.

He last saw her in March 2011, when she came to his residence to collect hair. He reported that this visit was uneventful.

On Friday, June 17th, 2011, he learnt via the social network *Facebook* that Julia was missing. On Saturday, June 18th, 2011, he learnt via his Blackberry service that a female body believed to be that of Julia was found near the airport.

He visited the scene and police officers there learnt that he was her former boyfriend and they invited him to Oistins police station to be interviewed. He gave an account of his whereabouts on June 13th. No discrepancies were found, and a check was also made of his white Toyota Corolla. However, nothing suspicious was found.

Lloyd Walmer

Another man, Lloyd Walmer was interviewed by police in June 2011. He met Julia while she was working at a financial services company, where he also worked. Over time, they exchanged contact information and became sexually involved in 2010. He told police that he and Julia last had an intimate relationship in January 2011. They would also go out to nightclubs and party, and he would sometimes transport her friends to and from these functions. He remained friendly with her and learnt from her that she was involved in ambivalent sexual relationships with a police officer and a deejay between December 2010 and May 2011. Ryan, the deejay was her boyfriend at the time. Julia told him about her relationship with Ryan and his actions towards her, including violent behaviour.

Lloyd stated that he last saw Julia on June 10th, 2011, when they went to a nightclub, accompanied by her friend, Yvonne. After attending the club, he was taking her home when they had a disagreement and they both got out of his car near Paynes Bay. He wanted to rekindle the relationship, but Julia deleted him from her Blackberry Messenger. He later learnt that she was missing from friends.

He provided police with an account of his whereabouts on June 13th, 2011 and the police found no discrepancies. Police also checked his motor car and nothing unusual was found. He gave a sample of his blood to Dr. Herbert for DNA analysis, and this was submitted to the Forensic Science Centre.

Jonathan Brathwaite

Jonathan Brathwaite, a police officer, told the police investigators that he knew the victim for over a year. They would see each other at various party locations and eventually became friends. They exchanged contact information and he visited her residence occasionally. They became sexually involved during February 2011, and Julia told friends that he was her boyfriend. He, however, did not consider her to be his girlfriend. He was involved in a vehicular accident around that time, and she gave him the majority of the money – $1,000.00 to repair his car.

During April 2011, they visited Sheraton Centre where he saw a woman that attended secondary school with him. They greeted each other, hugged, and kissed each other on the cheek. This infuriated Julia and it led to a dispute and a scuffle ensued between them. As a result, they spoke less frequently, and the relationship became less intense.

On two occasions, she invited him to a nightclub. He declined at first but later decided to visit the club without informing her. Whilst there, he saw her dancing very closely with a man who he recognised to be a deejay from the club. The man was caressing her, and he sent a Blackberry message to her, telling her he hoped she was enjoying herself. She saw him and came over and told him that it was nothing like that, suggesting that she was not involved with the deejay. He then left the club.

About a week later, Julia accidentally sent him a message which was meant for another man because it had the man's name. The message had words to the effect that it was nothing like that and they did not have to end.

As a result, Jonathan sent her a Blackberry message telling her that he had received the message meant for another man and that the truth had come out. He then deleted her contact information from his Blackberry.

He last saw her on May 20th, 2011, while he was on duty along Baxter's Road, and she was a passenger aboard a minibus. He received a cellphone call from her at the time. She also called him on June 8th, 2011, during which she inquired as to how he was and requested that he visit her. He however cut short the conversation and did not visit.

On June 12th, 2011, he received a Blackberry message from Julia asking him what he would have done if someone threatened him. However, she did not go into details. He told her that he would report the matter to the police.

On June 16th, 2011 he received a call from Sergeant Matthews from Holetown Police Station who enquired about Julia and told him that she had been reported missing by her mother. He gave an account of his whereabouts on June 13th. No discrepancies were found, and his motor car was checked and nothing unusual was found. He was asked to give a sample of his blood for DNA, which he voluntary gave to Dr Murray and this was submitted to the Government Analysis. There was no evidence linking him to the murder.

The police also interviewed Marlene, a close female friend of Julia. Marlene told the police that they often partied together and she believed she knew all the happenings in her life, even though she admitted that she did not know everything that happened with her.

She told investigators that Julia was in a relationship with Ryan Massiah who worked as a disc jockey at a nightclub. In the nightclub, she admitted that Julia would dance with other men, but if Ryan danced or talked to other women, she would argue with him. This often caused them to fight, whether physical or verbal, but usually physical. She said that on more than one occasion, Ryan beat Julia in the club. The first time that the beating took place was on May 20th, 2011 when she saw Ryan slap Julia beside her head. They did not discuss why the fight took place. That night he drove them home with his car.

The following week, May 27th, 2011, they returned to the club along with a friend named Cherisse and were partying. Ryan worked that night in the club, played the music and left. She went into the bathroom and on her return, she did not see Julia. She asked Cherisse for Julia and was told that Julia went outside to get fresh air. She spent another 15 minutes and Julia never returned. She contacted her on the phone and she told her that she was by a strip club.

Marlene and Cherisse went to the club and saw Julia outside, leaning on a wall outside the club. Ryan's car was also outside, and he emerged from the club and went towards his car. Julia moved off the wall and went towards Ryan' car as well. They were shouting at each other in an angry and aggressive tone and he told her to move. He was already sitting in his car at the time. The car engine was turned on at the time and Julia was reaching through the driver's side window of the car and Ryan drove off to the stoplights. The upper part of Julia's body was in the car, and Marlene could hear her heels dragging in the road. Ryan stopped the car, opened the door and pushed her off. She fell in the road. He got out of the car and they started to fight. Marlene said she saw him kick her while she was on the ground.

On Monday, May 13th 2011, Marlene was at home when Julia sent her a message saying she wanted a knife she had given to her. She had a knife when they were going to school and she took it from her to keep her out of trouble. She told her she wanted the knife because she had things to deal with. She came to her home and collected a silver bladed, black-handled knife with a clip on the side. She never asked her about the knife or if she used it or not.

On June 3rd, 2011 Julia and Marlene went to the nightclub. Ryan and Julia were in the club and she missed both of them for a while. When she returned, her face was swollen. She asked her about her face, but she refused to answer.

One week later, they returned to the nightclub. While in the club, everything appeared normal. An employee of the club was quarrelling about people standing in front of the fan. Julia was next to her and she went outside, leaving her in the club. After the club finished, Julia messaged her and told her to come and go home before she got into a fight. She asked her what happened and she did not answer. While outside, Julia said that the employee said that she, Julia, wanted to beat her for Ryan.

They left the area in Lloyd's car and were being taken home when he got angry and put them out of his car in Paynes Bay. It was usual for Julia to take the bus to Esso Black Rock and Ryan would collect her there. Whenever they partied in St Lawrence Gap, they would take the Oistins' bypass bus at midnight, and Julia would organise the transportation back home. Different people brought them home at night. Ryan never came to their home to pick them up to go partying, but he brought them home about five times.

On June 13th 2011, Julia told Marlene that she was in contact with another deejay and he asked her to be his girl. On June 20th, 2011, Marlene communicated with this deejay via Blackberry and he told her that what Julia said was not true. Marlene told the police that on many occasions, she had proven that Julia either withheld things from her or outright lied to her.

Ryan Massiah

Ryan Massiah was interviewed at Oistins Police Station for four days. He arrived at the station of his own volition, stating that he had come to assist in identifying Julia's body since he was the last person to see her alive (his own words). He was employed as a disc jockey at a nightclub for three years. He had a girlfriend at the time. He met Julia at the club during the early part of May 2011. She approached him, and they exchanged contact information and started to communicate via Blackberry messenger, and he met some of her friends. A few days after they met, he took her out. They soon started a sexual relationship, and this would usually occur in his motor car after the club closed at night. He stated that she began to exhibit behaviour which he did not approve of, namely consuming a lot of alcohol and gyrating on the ground at the club. He thought that this was below standard for any woman with whom he was involved since he sought to be seen as well poised. The police noted that he was very concerned about his physical appearance, manner of dress and acquaintances.

Julia also became very annoyed when she saw him talking to any women at the club and she got into verbal disputes with women he said were his friends. He was experiencing problems with his girlfriend, and he also learnt that Julia was telling persons that he was her boyfriend. He however only considered their relationship to be strictly sexual. This caused problems between them and eventually led to physical confrontations. He wanted to end the relationship, but she said she was pregnant for him. This reported pregnancy concerned him to the extent that he bought a pregnancy test with the intention that she use it for confirmation. He had no choice then but to tell his girlfriend about his relationship with Julia.

He told police that on Sunday, June 12th, 2011 he collected Julia from the Esso service station at Walmer Lodge, St Michael just after 7:00 p.m. He was driving his motor car and she was wearing a black and white dress with an animal skin pattern, red shoes, red belt and was carrying a red handbag. They went for a drive, from Black Rock to the south coast, then back to Bridgetown.

According to him, during his trip, he told her he wanted to end the relationship and she was begging him not to. He said that whilst travelling along Wharf Road, she went into her handbag to get money for bus fare, and he realised that there was a knife in her bag. He questioned her about being in possession of this knife and she told him that she had it for her protection. According to him, he managed to snatch the knife from her bag, examined it and returned it to her. He then took her to the Cheapside bus terminal where she got out of the car. This was between 8:00 p.m. and 9:00 p.m. She caught the bus while he returned to his residence.

On June 13th, 2011 he played music aboard a catamaran cruise between 3:00 p.m. and 8:00 p.m. and after that, he went home and slept until the following morning. He denied seeing or being in contact with Julia on June 13th, 2011.

He was kept in custody and his account was checked.

On the second day in custody, Ryan Massiah admitted that he had lied about his account of what happened that night. He then stated that on June 12th, 2011, Julia contacted him via Blackberry messenger and requested to see him, but he refused. She was threatening to come to his residence, and he believed she was going to cause a commotion. In addition, his girlfriend was at the house. She continued to message him about seeing her, so he agreed to meet her on June 13th. She told him that she would catch the 9:00 p.m. bus and they agreed to meet at the bus stop opposite the Esso Service station at Walmer Lodge. He collected her at 9:00 p.m. and she was wearing a white top, black leggings, black shoes and she was carrying a black purse.

He was wearing three-quarter pants and a checkered shirt and was barefooted. They took a drive and he later took her to the Cheapside bus stand to catch an 11:00 p.m. bus. According to him, the relationship was terminated that night. He did not see her off but returned to his home. He told the police that even though the relationship ended that night, he called her the following day but received no answer.

According to him, this was the last time he saw Julia. He told police that he had lied earlier because he was afraid as he was the last person to have been in the company of Julia and felt that he would have been accused of having something to do with her demise.

A check was made of his motor car using a light source and a presumptive blood test. Traces of blood were found on the front passenger seat and the rear seat. Massiah stated that about a month prior, he had sex in the front seat of his car with a woman named Amelia and she had a problem with vaginal bleeding. He could not explain the blood on the back seat, stating that he knew nothing about it. It was observed that Ryan Massiah had healed abrasions on his left shoulder, left forearm and left ear. He stated that he got the abrasions on his left forearm while shaving the said arm with a shaving machine. He could not explain how he got the other abrasions. These abrasions were examined by Dr Murray for investigative purposes. He stated that they could be one week to two weeks old. The abrasion on the shoulder could have been caused by a sharp object.

Amelia was interviewed and she confirmed that she had sex several times with Ryan in his car. She said that around May 9th, 2011, she had called Ryan for a ride home and on the way home, they stopped by Port St Charles to relax for a little bit and talked about his career and other things and they later had sex in the front passenger seat.

After the sex, Ryan took her home and when she got out of the car, she told him to check and see if she had left anything in the car. She saw Ryan using the light from his cellphone to check the car seat while she stood outside his motor car looking around because it was in the early hours of the morning. While doing so, Ryan said "You left blood in my seat," and asked her why was that. She responded and told him she did not know, it just happened. She then went inside the house and he drove off. That was the last time they had sex together or were out together, according to Amelia.

She said that the reason she asked Ryan to check the car seat to see if she left anything in it because inside the car was dark and she was constantly in and out of her bag and she did not want to lose any of her makeup or hair accessories and his cellphone was the only means of light in the car at the time.

She told the police that she had bled previous times after having sex with other partners because of having "rough sex" which caused her vaginal walls to be damaged.

After she heard of Julia's death, she called him, and he told her that he was at the police station, and he could not talk at that time and would call her back. He did not call her back, but he messaged her and told her that he was at the police station when she called, and that is why he could not talk. She asked him why he was there, and he told her that he went to the police station to identify the body and the Blackberry conversation ended, leaving her puzzled as to why he would have to go to the police station to identify Julia's body.

In light of that, a voluntary sample of her blood was obtained. The blood samples were submitted to the Government Analyst, Lorraine Alleyne of the Forensic Science Centre. Constable Grace took possession of the rear seat of the motor car for analysis. A check was also made of the Blackberry cellphone of Mr. Massiah but recent contact information was missing.

The police stated that his statement was thoroughly checked and there was no hardcore evidence to associate him with the murder. However, the findings of the blood analysis were never known. Further discussions of a forensic nature revealed that even if the blood at the back of the car was indeed identified as Julia's, there could be no arrest as the cause of death was unknown due to the advanced decomposition of the body.

The case of the death of Julia has been presented to you with the facts and statements of those who knew her and those who were with her up to the days and weeks leading to her death. Who killed Julia? Did the police interview the actual killer? Is the killer's statement part of this account? These are the burning questions.

CHAPTER ELEVEN

Discussion

These are the facts, circumstances, witness and police statements/ records, surrounding ten of Barbados' unsolved murders over the period 1970-2011. They are disturbing, shocking and brutal, and because the cases are *real* they may be painful to read.

The themes of gender-based violence and violence in general, drug abuse, drug trafficking, sex, prostitution and mental health issues, are central themes throughout these murder cases.

The discussion in this chapter seeks to unpack some of these themes in relation to the current state of cold cases and make recommendations on the way forward.

Lifestyles as a contributing factor

Victimology is *always* important when examining a homicide. It looks at the characteristics of the victim, their associates, lifestyles and most importantly, whether they may have been involved in activities that contributed to their demise.

According to research and typologies on victims by theorists such as Mendelsohn (1956), there are different types of victims, including some who are innocent to their victimization. Such victims were just unfortunate victims of homicide. Many victims do fall into this category.

Regretfully, however, some victims have lifestyles that make them vulnerable to victimization. For example, persons who are involved in the drug trade often place themselves at risk due to the nature of the trade. Greed, jealousy, turf wars, and other factors lead to violence. Other lifestyle factors such as the subculture of the streets, associations and gang affiliation also predispose persons to lives of crime.

Gender-Based Violence

Violence against women is one of the main themes emerging from this book. The degradation of women, seen through incidences of physical, verbal and sexual abuse is boldly on display. The case of Andrea Brathwaite,

Mark Swenson's girlfriend and other cases in the book highlight the cycle of abuse.

Gender-based violence (GBV) or violence against women and girls (VAWG), is a global pandemic that affects 1 in 3 women in their lifetime.

The statistics are alarming:

- One in three women worldwide have experienced either physical and/or sexual intimate partner violence or non-partner sexual violence.

- Globally, 7% of women have been sexually assaulted by someone other than a partner.

- 38% of all murders of women are committed by an intimate partner.

In 2017, the United Nations Office on Drugs and Crime (UNODC) documented that worldwide, almost 6 out of 10 or 58 per cent of women intentionally killed are murdered by an intimate partner or other family member. GBV in the Caribbean is among the highest in the world and VAWG undermines women's position in Caribbean societies and perpetuates dangerous stereotypes of manhood.

According to UN Women, violence against women and girls is a global pandemic of alarming proportions, deeply rooted in gender inequality and discrimination. They also report that between 15 and 76% of women are targeted for physical and/or sexual violence in their lifetime, with most occurring within intimate relationships, as can be evidenced in these cases in this book.

Addressing and reducing intimate partner violence is problematic. It is mostly underreported, and even when brought to the attention of the criminal justice system, does not result in a conviction in most cases and for many reasons. We have seen in this book, instances where women have been ridiculed, sexually abused, badly beaten and set on fire. In many cases similar to those in this book, the women – having endured these violent acts – stayed in the abusive relationships. The main reasons for choosing to remain despite the abuse are fear, embarrassment and dependency.

The stark truth is that many women who have tried to leave such abusive relationships were killed in the process. Barbados and the Caribbean in general continue to struggle with the high incidences of violence perpetrated against women, not only in Barbados but throughout the region and globally. Regionally, In the past year alone, scores of women have been killed by their current or former partners – some in horrifically gruesome circumstances.

Domestic violence experts speak about the stages of the cycle of abuse. These cycles have been displayed in a few of the cases mentioned in this book. The first stage is the *tension-building stage*, where the abused person can sense that the dynamics of the relationship have changed negatively and that the strain is building and about to come to a head – the crisis stage. The honeymoon phase of the relationship is over and the arguments start; the atmosphere is always tense and filled with anxiety; the person starts being cautious, trying not to cause the abuser to start to abuse them. Some people refer to it as *walking on eggshells* around the abuser. It can last from hours to months.

The second stage is the actual incident of abuse, where the abuser unleashes their anger or frustration onto the abused party. This includes verbal, physical, psychological or sexual abuse. During this stage, the abuser may neglect or deny the victim's rights to basic things including access to their family and friends.

The third stage is the *honeymoon phase*. This is *not* to be confused with the "honeymoon phase" mentioned above in stage 1. This is what happens *after* the abuse. The abuser cries, begs for forgiveness, showers affections on the abused person and mollifies with gifts and promises that it will not happen again. Many abused persons react to the lavish attention of this second 'honeymoon' and forgive their abusers...until it happens again.

In some situations, women do not want to accept that what is happening to them *is* abuse, that it is illegal and should be reported. Fear, embarrassment, an unwillingness to engage the criminal justice system and dependency on the partner (manifesting partly in not wanting to get the person in trouble with the law) are some of the major factors why these crimes, for the most part, go unreported and undetected.

Further, in the case of sexual assault, there has been until recently, a firmly entrenched cultural tendency to blame women for their victimization in domestic relationships. Women who remain in such abusive relationships can be labelled as sick, crazy or accused of bringing the victimization on themselves and if they attempt to flee the abuse, they may find few supports and insufficient sympathy and empathy available.

The Barbadian society needs to do more to tackle and arrest the problem of gender based violence (GBV). We should continue to educate both men and women about GBV violence and issues of gender equality, and ensure that the degradation of women, so widely accepted to some degree across West Indian culture, generally, is staunched and extinguished for good.

The link between prostitution and violence

Prostitution is a risky activity in which GBV seems ever-present. The likelihood of female sex workers being robbed, assaulted, raped and/or murdered is far greater than the average woman. This is due in part to the nature of the 'work' and also the numbers and varieties of people with whom they come into contact on a regular basis: robbers, serial predators, drug dealers, *pimps*, customers and even passersby (Carmen & Moody, 1985; Dalla, 2002; Inciardi, 1993; Inciardi & Surratt, 2001; Maher, 1997; Miller, 1986; Teets, 1997).

Numerous studies have documented that although sex workers are victimized by a variety of different types of perpetrators, most of the violence they experience comes from their own customers, or dates (Church, Henderson, Barnard, & Hart, 2001; Coston & Ross, 1998; Davis, 2000). Many of them also experience a continuing cycle of violence throughout their lives. Many of these women have experienced violence or other forms of trauma at an early age and many resort to the use of drugs to numb the pain of the psychologically damaging experiences. In the cases covered in this book, the sex workers were addicted to hard core drugs such as cocaine and both met violent ends. The substantial levels of drug use and sex work engaged in by these women are often associated with violent encounters in their daily lives. Research conducted by Kurtz and Surratt (2004), highlighted that many of the prostitutes in the study gave historical self-reports of trauma experienced as children and adolescents.

One prostitute in the study stated, "It's like there are two worlds, there's a good world and then there's a violent world and it's like all we know is violence, all we know is violent men."

Moreira and Monteiro (2012) argued that the type of environment in which prostitutes operate also make them more vulnerable as, in the street, she is subject to arbitrary abuse from the police, pimps and clients. Among the various risks are those related to aggression: physical and sexual abuse, trafficking of women, rapes, robberies, insults and curses, and murder. Violence, according to them, was a near-constant in their industry.

The researchers noted that there are several policy and research implications of these findings. First, because women who use drugs, and are sex workers are so marginalized, some type of advocacy is warranted, – advocacy in terms of promoting a safer work environment and providing access to mental and physical health care, among other safety nets.

Second, mechanisms need to be established that serve to provide sex workers with alternatives to the street. Virtually all of the women encountered in this project indicated that prostitution is not a chosen or preferred career. Rather, for most, it is *survival* sex, and for the majority, it is the result of a drug habit combined with the lack of other skills or resources.

Or as one sex worker indicated: "When you need the cracks [crack cocaine] and you need money for other things 'cause your rent money went on the boards [was used to buy crack], you got to survive, and you know, to do that, the pussy works!"

The creation of alternatives to the street for this demographic, however, is not an easy task. Long-term substance abuse treatment plans that include strategies for the development of positive self-images and empowerment is only the beginning. In addition, there is the need for vocational education and the introduction to networks that will enable women to use their newly developed skills rather than their sexuality to support themselves.

Drugs and Violence

The relationship between violence and drugs is two-fold. First, there is enough evidence and in local cases to suggest that violence can be – and is – perpetrated under the influence of substances. Secondly, violence related to substance abuse stems from the drug trade and its operations.

Violence as a result of drug abuse

It has been well documented that violence and drug abuse are inextricably linked. Substance abuse can lead to aggression, particularly violent sex crimes. What is of interest is that violence is a two-way street, meaning that those who abuse substances are also likely to be met with violence, and a substantial number of persons who engage in violent crimes have a history of substance abuse or were under the influence at the time of the offence.

Studies have also found that highly addictive drugs such as methamphetamine and cocaine, when combined with low impulse control can lead persons to engage in high-risk behaviours and violent or aggressive sexual acts including rape and sexual assault.

In this book, we have seen a few cases where persons became addicted to drugs, stemming from a traumatic incident or experience in their lives. Research tells us that many survivors of trauma turn to drugs or alcohol to find relief from the physical and/or psychological pain remaining post-trauma. When left unaddressed, the pain becomes worse leading to behaviours and activities to numb the pain. As addiction takes hold, another problem is added to the cycle of substance abuse.

Violence as a result of the drug trade

One of the driving factors of person-on-person violence is the drug trade. The drug trade is a business in organised crime. The Caribbean's geographic location is a contributing factor to the presence of the drug trade in the region, as its positioning between the suppliers of illegal drugs and the consumers of illegal drugs, makes it a viable trans-shipment point.

According to UNODC 2008, the Caribbean region suffers from the world's highest murder rates, and research by UNODC and the World Bank highlights that drug trafficking is responsible for the rising rates of homicide and gun proliferation.

Disputes and turf wars between traffickers within the illegal drug markets often lead to violence and homicide. These disputes and wars are part of the subculture of violence. The general model of such a subculture is one characterised by "dense concentrations of socio-economically disadvantaged persons with few legitimate avenues of social mobility, lucrative illegal markets for forbidden goods and services, a value system that rewards only survival and material success, and private enforcement of the informal rules of the game" (Gottesman & Brown, 1999, p. 297).

Drug transactions go through a distribution chain and according to research, each link of this chain, each transaction, has the potential of resulting in a homicide. The further up the chain someone in the drug trade is involved, the homicide becomes more and more professionally executed. According to the US Department of Justice, the likelihood that a perpetrator is apprehended for homicide decreases as the professionalism of the 'hitmen' employed to do the killing increases. The fee is paid on completion of the contract. Implicitly understood in the contract is that if the killer is apprehended, he does not "give up," that is, inform on the person who hired him. If he does, he becomes the subject of a future contract.

What are some of the main factors in the drug trade that lead to homicide? According to police: stealing, disloyalty and jealousy are the most common explanations for most drug related murders on the island.

Stealing

Many persons within the drug trade are killed for stealing drugs from the drug trafficker or dealer.

Drugs are often distributed for sale on consignment. The drug dealer gives the supplier a certain amount of drugs on consignment, but in some situations, the person receiving the drugs on consignment does not pay back the stipulated amount. Failure to pay for the drugs often leads to the murder of the offender.

In addition, persons in or on the periphery of the trade, may hear of a landing of drugs and steal the drugs for resale on the market. Such persons are placing themselves in serious peril of death. Drug owners do not take theft lightly for to do so would be to lose not just the value of the drugs but, more importantly, respect. Embezzlement is also grounds for murder. For example, a dealer may have been given $20,000 in drugs to sell for the drug trafficker. He only brings back $10,000 and keeps the rest of the money for himself. Once discovered, that dealer's life is forfeit.

Disloyalty

Within the gang or group is a hierarchy, a defined rank structure. There is the leader and his lieutenants or soldiers. Some of these lieutenants or soldiers, in an attempt to cut out the leader, will go directly to the supplier of the drugs, purporting to be acting on behalf of the leader, and will divert business away from the leader to themselves. On other occasions, they will go to work with another drug dealer. Still others will try to elevate themselves by attempting to make more money than their original 'boss' or try to break away to form their own drug trafficking business. These scenarios are all viewed as acts of disloyalty and in the drug business, 'heads roll' for disloyalty.

Jealousy

The drug trade is a very competitive business that is fraught with jealousy. Lives are lost in the drug trade due to this jealousy. Drug dealers will watch each other's turf, money and other material possessions to gauge their own worth and jealousy flares easily at any perceived shortcoming. Plans are then made to redress the imbalance – turfs might be muscled in on, money and material possessions taken away. 'Hits' might even be issued to remove rivals in this most competitive of business undertakings.

Cold Cases

There are a substantial number of unsolved cases in Barbados over a window of approximately 40 years. These go back as far as the unsolved murder of Victor '*Pele*' Parris in 1978 up to more recent homicides within the past few years. Many homicides are not solved immediately and may take months and even years to bring a perpetrator to justice. In some cases, as highlighted in this book, they are never solved.

Additionally, not every person who is arrested and brought before the courts for murder is convicted. Some are released for lack of evidence or technicalities in law among other factors. In those cases, the families of the murdered victims often do not get the closure they desire. In their opinion, the perpetrator has not been punished. For the police, however, they considered the case closed, even though the courts have not convicted anyone. How can the police and the courts be on different pages? This anomaly affects families most as they continue to believe there is no closure.

It is important to acknowledge that the Royal Barbados Police Force is under-resourced, and this will naturally affect units such as a Cold Case Unit. A senior police official noted that the Cold Case Unit had to shift priorities in recent years as a result of an increase in certain crimes, particularly gun-related crimes. However, they do not see cold cases as 'cold', but rather these cases will be revisited as new information comes to the attention of the Force.

As was mentioned earlier, every cold case represents a person who has not received justice for the crime committed against them.

There is evidence in research on factors that make cases more or less likely to be solved. Some of these factors include whether it was recent (although "recent" is relative), if it did not involve a drug user and whether the victim was young. These make the cases more difficult to crack. Research suggests that if cold-case investigators are diligent about developing *new* theories of the crime, this aids in the clearance of cold cases.

Gun-related homicides are also harder to solve. This is largely due to the nature of many of these gun-related homicides, along with the fact that witnesses or persons who are knowledgeable about these crimes do not like to talk due to fear of reprisals. It is crucial that the culture of reporting crimes is changed.

Current challenges in investigating homicides and other serious crimes

According to the RBPF, it is challenged because society has changed. Information from eyewitnesses – known as "I see" witnesses – have perennially been the lifeline of investigations. However, in recent years the number and availability of these witnesses have been dropping. Why? As discussed earlier, genuine fear of reprisals and an aversion to the "snitching mentality" are the main reasons for the trend. Murder-accused are now being released on bail, along with their cohorts. There is also an increased and concerning level of boldness of criminality – including public and daylight shootings of persons and this development has had an adverse effect on the willingness of witnesses to come forward and testify.

There are still people who want to assist in investigations but do not want to testify or give official statements to the police. The police have noted that legislation in other jurisdictions allows witnesses to give official statements without coming to court. This type of witness is called a 'confidential informant'. The issue in Barbados is that an accused person has the right, by law, to confront a witness face-to-face.

Another challenge relates to identification parades. People can identify an accused person through an identification parade, but based on the current set-up of face-to-face lineups, people are unwilling to 'ID' anyone for fear of reprisals. The police have implemented one-way mirrors in some police stations, but some people do not trust them and there is still the nagging reality that witnesses have to present themselves at court and confront the accused.

Barbados has no witness protection programme and the two key features that would have to be considered if such a programme were to be implemented, are the cost and logistics of starting a new life in another country. Further, due to the small size of the island, a witness protection programme is not feasible and basically pointless.

With all of these challenges, it is imperative that the focus shifts to forensic science as the key to solving cases, and away from the great reliance on eyewitness testimony. With this knowledge, the RBPF has begun to focus on science, especially in the area of ballistics, but many more elements of forensic science must be explored and embraced to aid in improving the crime-solving rate.

Reinstatement of the Cold Case Unit

It is recommended that the Cold Case Unit be reinstated, rebranded and maintained with new energy. This will give the families and friends some reassurance that their loved ones have not been forgotten.

The needs of the Unit should first be established in terms of resources: number of investigators, other staff, building, equipment etc. There must be capacity building for investigators in the form of training. Resources should be focused on these cases solely with a cap on the number of cases under each investigator.

An electronic register of all cold cases should be created going back as far as the 1980s. Information on their statuses, leads, witnesses, suspects and all other relevant details would form part of the database

For best results, different investigators should be assigned to the Unit to examine these cases. A former police officer stressed that sometimes it is important for 'new eyes' to review old cases as they may detect something that the other investigators were unable to detect. This strategy allows investigators to review all of the evidence, look for missing leads and see whether different approaches, forensic approaches or new witnesses should be utilised.

Most important is the need to communicate with victims, once alive. This Unit should give regular updates to victims' families and should consider working alongside the Victim Support Unit with social workers when communicating with the families.

Development of a cold case programme on television

Consideration should be given to revisiting the Crime Scene television series where unresolved cases would be reenacted to the public with the modus operandi, giving information on when and where they occurred and asking the public's assistance in helping the police to solve these cases.

In conclusion, there is a lot of work to be done. Violent crime continues to be a major concern for all, especially violence against women. Physical and sexual abuse, degradation, neglect, sexual objectification and the exertion of control and dominance over women have been recurring themes in this book.

The drug trade has also been linked to several homicides over the years, including some unsolved murders. People involved in the drug trade knowingly put their lives in danger, risking death, injury or incarceration for the sake of lucre. There is need for increased public awareness about the dangers of drug trafficking and drug use.

I wish to close by saying that in every murder, someone always sees or knows something.

Is that someone *you*?